AT THE POINT

THE BODY

SAYS NO

All that you need to know on how to beat stress

By

Lynda H. Parker

Table of Contents

Introduction

How might this benefit me? Comprehend the reason why stress is so impeding to your health.

How might you respond assuming a companion called to let you know she was in horrifying agony that left her unfit to walk? Could you call her powerless and advise her to simply disregard it? Or on the other hand, could you demand that she go to the clinic - and maybe even take her there yourself? Undoubtedly, you'd adopt the last strategy. In any case, imagine a scenario in which the tables were turned, and you were the one encountering that equivalent extreme aggravation.

A considerable lot of us like to keep up with the fact that we're solid, even indestructible. We persuade ourselves that we can deal with any measure of physical or profound agony, either by subduing it, disregarding it, or obsessing about others' concerns, all things being equal.

Yet, this approach essentially doesn't work. It jeopardizes our health, and it covers our internal shortcomings. By denying our concerns, we try not to address them. Our bodies over and again tell us no, yet we will not tune in - until it's past the point of no return. It's about time we stood up to the basic reasons for our ailments and assumed back command over our health.

In this book, you'll learn

- How injury can twist your "hunches"

- Why individuals with ALS are so great; and
- The explanation: it's great to think adversely now and again.

CHAPTER ONE

Stress and the actual impacts on your body

It is widely known that an overburden of stress isn't sound and can inconveniently affect your psychological and actual well-being.

Dr Morgan Mkhatshwa, Clinical Leader at Bonitas Clinical Asset, examines how an excessive amount of stress obstructs the ideal working of your body and brain and results in a disturbing number of medical problems.

What is stress?

Stress is a characteristic human reaction to difficulties and dangers in our lives.

It normally happens when we are in a circumstance that we don't feel we can oversee or control.

Medicinally, stress causes compound changes in the body that can raise your circulatory strain, pulse, and glucose levels.

Anyway, what befalls your body?

Your Sensory Nervous System (SNS) is an organization of nerves that assists your body with enacting its 'instinctive' reaction.

This framework's movement builds when you're worried, at serious risk, or actually dynamic.

The body moves its energy assets toward fending off apparent life danger or escaping from a foe. The SNS flags the adrenal organs to deliver chemicals called adrenalin (epinephrine) and cortisol.

- The battle reaction is your body's approach to confronting any apparent danger forcefully.
- Flight implies your body urges you to run from risk.
- Freeze is your body's failure to move or act against a danger.

Research recommends that stress likewise can welcome or deteriorate specific side effects or illnesses.

What are the most widely recognized actual side effects in response to stress?

The cortisol and adrenaline chemicals delivered during a distressing circumstance can cause a few changes in your body, including:

- **Expanded pulse and circulatory strain:** The expanded degree of chemicals can make your heart beat quicker and your veins tighten, prompting worse hypertension.

- **Stomach-related issues:** Stress can influence your stomach-related framework and cause side effects, for example, stomach torment, bulging, obstruction, or loose bowels.

- **Debilitated safe framework:** Constant stress can smother your insusceptible framework and make you more vulnerable to diseases and sicknesses.

- **Muscle strain and agony:** Stress can cause muscle stress and torment, particularly in your neck, shoulders, and back.

- **Cerebral pains:** Stress can set off strain migraines, headaches as well, and strong fits in the neck and shoulders.

- **Rest issues:** Stress can obstruct your rest, causing trouble nodding off, staying unconscious, or getting up too soon.

- **Skin issues:** Stress can intensify skin conditions like dermatitis, psoriasis, or skin inflammation.

- **Endocrine issues:** brought about by stress incorporate thyroid chemicals prompting hyperthyroidism or hypothyroidism, ghrelin and leptin, the chemicals that manage craving, expanding hunger, melatonin, bringing about anxiety and a sleeping disorder, insulin, adding to Type 2 diabetes.

- **Psychological wellness issues:** Persistent stress can likewise add to the advancement of emotional health problems, for example, nervousness, despondency, and wearout.

How would you screen your feelings of anxiety?

To screen your stress, first distinguish your stress triggers.

What drives you to feel crazy, tense, stressed, or crabby?

Do you frequently get migraines or an irritated stomach with no clinical reason?

Is it hard to concentrate or do you experience difficulty resting around evening time?

Generally speaking, constant stress can add to the turn of events or deterioration of ongoing circumstances like diabetes, heftiness, discouragement, and uneasiness. Stress can be an executioner. Which is the reason dealing with your stress is fundamental.

Do this through solid ways of dealing with especially difficult times like activity, reflection, profound breathing, or looking for proficient assistance, if important.

Furthermore, recall, your General Practitioner ought to be your most memorable port to meet all your medical care needs.

We accept there should be coordination of care and urge you to see your General Practitioner, who can refer you to a trained professional or helper supplier as needs be.

Tips to adapt to Stress the healthy way

Can we just be real for a moment, life is brimming with huge stressors and circumstances that can burden us both intellectually and genuinely. Here are a few hints to adapt to stress solidly.

Stress is a Pandemic

Stress has become such a shared characteristic in our general public that it is practically expected, undeniable, and unmanageable. Further, assuming we get some margin to self-look at, one can contend that living with stress has become to a lesser extent a battle to cure and a greater amount of an undeniable encounter to just "adapt" with. The American Foundation for Stress reports that generally, 73% of individuals concur that stress influences their emotional wellness, while practically 40% say stress is totally overpowering.

Stress Influences Others In an Unexpected Way

Considering the reality of stress, it's anything but a one-size-fits-all variable for everybody. While some are normally more delicate to stress and adapt to it, others are normally more "versatile" at the time. This is because of different elements, like disposition contrasts, character qualities, childhood, and acclimation. In any case, this doesn't imply that the drawn-out impacts of stress (particularly delayed stress) are not as yet common. We as a whole need tips to adapt to stress in a sound and useful ways and can profit from careful practices in different circumstances.

Tips to Adapt to Stress

- **Self-face knead:** We should begin with an actual arrangement! While parting from a high-stress circumstance, begin by rubbing your sanctuaries with your file and pointer for 1-2 minutes. Do likewise to your temple and facial structure, remaining as loose as could be expected.

- **Distinguish high-stress triggers:** The facts confirm that staying away from unpleasant circumstances, by and large, is inescapable. Be that as it may, distinguish what circumstances, happenings, conditions, or triggers bring about a delayed negative response to said stressor and layout limits and backing inside them.

- **Limit specific energizers:** On the off chance that you distinguish as being exceptionally worried and have encountered deteriorating mental or actual side effects from said stress, keeping away from specific energizers is a sound road of mending and adapting (notwithstanding friend or expert help).

- **Practice care:** Breathing activities, yoga, regular breaks during the day, and, surprisingly, certain versatile applications with careful updates are simple apparatuses to execute care rehearses in your everyday daily schedule.

- **Interface with various local area roads:** Most know the advantages of local area and association. Notwithstanding, it is essential to develop different outlets of the local area and the connections inside them, one of which being the work environment.

- **Focus on actual well-being:** From a week-after-week workout everyday practice to eating less carbs and particularly sound rest, actual health assumes a significant part in stress reaction and filtration.

CHAPTER TWO

Mental Fatigue

Mental Fatigue: What Is It And How To Conquer It?

If you battle to get up following a strong night's rest and fear your essential regular undertakings, you might be managing mental weariness. Maybe work has been more difficult than expected, you've been focusing on a wiped-out family member, or you have disregarded taking care of yourself. Be that as it may, there is some uplifting news: you can find straightforward ways to defeat mental fatigue and return to your old, vivacious self.

What Does Being Intellectually Depleted Mean?

Mental depletion happens when you experience outrageous weariness and show indications of aloofness, skepticism, and. After managing long-haul stress, you can find it hard to zero in on your undertakings or partake in your exercise. These progressions might demonstrate that you are intellectually or sincerely depleted.

It is normal to encounter weakness, both truly and intellectually. Nonetheless, drawn-out and ignored mental weariness can influence mental capacities, critical thinking abilities, and close-to-home control. This can bring about huge difficulties in your everyday schedule and connections.

Side Effects of Mental Fatigue

Mental and actual depletion are both normal events, particularly in our quick-moving present-day way of life. In any case, perceiving the early side effects of mental weariness is significant in beating this issue and returning to your standard efficiency levels. Moving right along, we should dive into the physical, profound, and conduct indications of mental exhaustion.

Actual Side effects

The most observable side effects of mental weariness are actual ones, for example,

- Actual weariness and weakness, in spite of getting a quality night's rest.
- Migraines, muscle strain, and body throbs.

- Rest aggravations and changes in rest design.
- Loss of craving.
- Stomach throb and stomach-related uneasiness.
- Sporadic heartbeat.
- Hypertension.
- Successive colds.

Profound Side effects

Mental weariness is likewise described by striking profound changes, including:

- Loss of interest in regular exercises and cherished leisure activities.
- Absence of inspiration in your expert life.
- Absence of direction in your own life and ill humor.

- Negativity, criticism, and self-question
- Relentless stress.
- A waiting inclination that something terrible will occur.

Social Side effects

At last, mental depletion causes a great many conduct changes, for example,

- Anxiety and failure to unwind.
- Self-seclusion and withdrawal from social exercises.
- Inconvenience zeroing in on undertakings, carelessness, stalling.
- Attacking relatives, companions, or colleagues.
- Expanded inclination toward risk-taking ways of behaving.

- Undesirable methods for dealing with especially difficult times, for example, liquor or illicit drug use.

How To Fix Mental Exhaustion?

There are various ways of lessening mental depletion. Changing your way of life can assist you with handling it from the root, while survival techniques can assist you with feeling revived and restored while managing upsetting circumstances. Here are the fundamental stages to take in the event of mental fatigue.

Have a go at Getting More Rest

Getting sufficient quality rest is fundamental for your actual prosperity and in general well-being, including mental and close-to-home well-being. Getting the ideal 7 to 8 hours of rest every night decreases both mental and actual weariness.

Take out Stressors

At the point when the stress of regular daily existence overpowers you, make a move right away and feel free to ask for help. We as a whole vibe are overpowered by work liabilities occasionally, however in the event that the stress becomes terrible, you ought to ask your boss or a collaborator for help. Likewise, assuming you experience weakness connected with providing care or family errands, consider depending on your relatives or companions. Some of the time, it's difficult to kill stress triggers from your life, yet doing so is the most ideal way to keep away from mental weariness and burnout.

Enjoy some time off

Taking a respite and allowing yourself to unwind and recapture energy can essentially assist with diminishing mental depletion. A break can allude to any of the following things:

Going on a drawn out vacation

- Investing an hour of energy in taking care of oneself exercises consistently
- Eliminating unimportant errands from your daily agenda

- Getting the best out of your midday break (for instance, leaving the workplace for an entire hour and taking a flavorful dinner, a walk, or one more loosening up action beyond work)
- Investing quality energy with companions no less than one time per week, (for example, eating or watching motion pictures together)

Last Consideration

Albeit mental weariness is a staggering encounter that impedes our day-to-day routines, it isn't super durable. With sufficient taking care of oneself methodologies and backing from your friends and family, you can defeat mental exhaustion and flourish in each part of your life once more.

CHAPTER THREE

Overpowered

What's the significance here of Feel Overpowered?

Do you feel like you have such a lot going on that you're battling to adapt to everything? Or on the other hand, would you say you are going through something upsetting that is making it challenging for you to work? These are a portion of the indications of being overpowered.

At the point when overpowered, an individual is overflowed by considerations, feelings, and actual sensations — frequently connected with a particular issue — that can be challenging for them to make due, says

Sabrina Romanoff, PsyD, a clinical clinician and teacher at Yeshiva College.

Everybody feels overpowered occasionally and it is a totally common reaction to regular stressors, says Dr. Romanoff. Stress can here and there be useful, on the grounds that it starts up your framework and assists you with being more useful. Nonetheless, being persistently worried and continually feeling overpowered can negatively affect your psychological and actual well-being.

This article investigates the side effects and reasons for feeling overpowered, as well as some methods for dealing with hardship or stress that might be useful.

Signs and Side Effects of Being Overpowered

These are a portion of the signs that you're overpowered, as per Dr. Romanoff:

- **Nonsensical contemplations:** You might battle to think sanely, which can cause the issue to appear to be swelled and your apparent capacity to manage it feels empty.

- **Loss of motion:** You might encounter a freeze reaction that can make you feel deadened and unfit to work. Indeed, even straightforward errands can feel inconceivable. You might wind up deferring distressing errands, or keep away from them through and through.

- **Unbalanced responses:** You might go overboard to minor stressors. For example, you might overreact assuming that you can't track down your keys.
- **Withdrawal:** You might end up pulling out from loved ones. You might feel like they can't help you or comprehend what you're going through.
- **Cynicism:** You might have a powerless and miserable outlook on the circumstance.
- **Mind-set transforms:** You might feel irate, bad-tempered, or restless, and cry without any problem.
- **Mental exhaustion:** You might feel confused and experience issues

concentrating, deciding, and taking care of issues.

- **Actual side effects:** You might encounter actual side effects, for example, quick heartbeat, trouble breathing, dazedness, weariness, migraines, squeezes, an irritated stomach, or different throbbing painfulness.

Being constantly anxious and overpowered can prompt physical and psychological wellness conditions, for example, hypertension, coronary illness, corpulence, wretchedness, tension, and fixation.

It is overpowered to Adapt

Beneath, Dr. Romanoff shares a few systems that can assist you with adapting, assuming you're feeling overpowered.

Alter Your Viewpoint

Make a stride back from your manners of thinking. Perceive and acknowledge how you are feeling and the circumstances you are in. Stop the horrendous profound pattern of rumination.

Give your very best to get some point of view on the circumstance. You can have a go at enjoying some time off from the circumstance, taking a walk, changing your current circumstance, addressing a companion, or taking a couple of full breaths.

Search our assets to assist you with tackling the issue. This could mean requesting help, doing something to recalibrate your point of view, or moving toward the issue from an alternate point.

Challenge Your Presumptions

At the point when we're overpowered, we will generally let silly considerations and fears guide us, rather than being consistent. For example, in the event that you're going through a separation, you might stress over what individuals might think about you, or you might fret over being single and winding up alone.

It tends to be useful to distinguish irrational suspicions and eloquent them, so you can look at them in the radiance of the day and see that they aren't guaranteed to turn out as expected. You can have a go at thinking of them down in a diary or voicing them without holding back to somebody you trust. Connect with your socially encouraging group of people. Your companions, family, and partners might have the option to offer counsel, support, and an alternate point of view.

Acknowledge the assistance of your friends and family and leave them alone there for you. Indeed, even conversing with steady individuals in your day-to-day existence can assist you with feeling more secure and more approved with regard to the stressor.

Attempt Care Activities

Care can be exceptionally useful while you're feeling overpowered. Establishing procedures like the 5-4-3-2-1 activity utilizes your faculties to associate you with your current circumstance and assist you with escaping the bedlam of your brain.

You can play out the 5-4-3-2-1 activity by sitting in a peaceful spot and seeing things around you. Attempt to list:

- 5 things you can see
- 4 things you can contact or feel
- 3 things you can hear
- 2 things you can smell
- 1 thing you can taste

This exercise can help you quiet down and step away from the staggering considerations and feelings you're encountering. You can utilize it to have some time off and reapproach the issue later according to a new viewpoint.

See a Specialist

Treatment can assist you with fostering the abilities you want to deal with the sensations of being overpowered. It likewise can assist you with understanding the reason why you will generally have areas of strength for this to stressors, especially in the event that you have a background marked by feeling overpowered.

Treatment can likewise assist you with tracking down ways of expanding certainty through skill, the two of which decidedly build up one another — the more equipped you are, the more sure you feel, as well as the other way around.

Something From Verywell

Assuming that you're managing something upsetting, you might begin to feel overpowered and experience issues adapting. You might end up ruminating over the issue continually and feeling frozen or deadened. You might try and begin to feel wiped out and encounter other actual side effects.

On the off chance that you're feeling overpowered, it may very well be useful to have some time off from the issue, get some point of view on it, converse with your friends and family about it, and afterward return to it while you're feeling far improved. Treatment can likewise be a wellspring of help that can assist you with figuring out your response and foster adapting abilities to manage it.

Motivations behind Why You Might Feel Overpowered

An encouraging stressor, a surprising occasion, or poor emotional wellness can make you feel overpowered, says Dr. Romanoff. She makes sense that you may likewise feel overpowered assuming a progression of stressors gather and heap onto you. An absence of adapting abilities can likewise worsen side effects.

These are a portion of the normal triggers that can make you feel overpowered, as per Dr. Romanoff:

- Loss of a friend or family member
- Exorbitant responsibility or an unpleasant workplace
- Struggle in private associations with companions or relatives
- Relationship troubles or separations
- Monetary issues

- Wellbeing concerns
- Horrible encounters
- Natural or policy-driven issues
- Significant life-altering event

Having an emotional wellness condition, for example, melancholy, nervousness, post-traumatic stress disorder issue (PTSD), or fanatical habitual problem (OCD) could incline an individual toward feeling overpowered, says Dr. Romanoff.

CHAPTER FOUR

Stress Management's Strategies I

Enjoying some time off from work is fundamental, but many individuals leave their downtime unused.1 Whether you plan a getaway, a staycation, or a playcation, it's crucial to have some time off from your work, your daily schedule, and the requests of life to hold feelings of anxiety within proper limits.

At the point when you have some time off, you're not evading liability. You're dealing with yourself so you'll have the endurance to be your best. By learning the signs that you want a break, you'll know when to plan some time away to assist you with feeling invigorated and re-established.

Initially

Enjoying some time off from work is imperative to overstress and stay balanced. Signs that you could have to enjoy some time off incorporate the inclination skeptical, depleted, or removed. By having some time off, whether it's a vacation or simply a brief break during the day, you can return to your work with a fresher, more refreshed mind.

Dangers of Not Enjoying Reprieves

The body is intended to answer short eruptions of stress. At the point when stress is drawn out and the stress reaction is set off over and over and routinely — as can occur in a distressing position or a contention-ridden relationship — the circumstance transforms into one of constant stress, and genuine medical conditions can set in.

Persistent stress might make you more helpless to conditions going from continuous migraines and gastrointestinal issues to hypertension, which brings an expanded gamble of coronary illness and stroke.

When your allostatic burden, or generally speaking degree of stress, gathers to a specific level, stress can accelerate on the grounds that you're continually in a condition of reactivity.

Right now, even good occasions can feel overpowering assuming they take energy to appreciate. You're not ready to answer from a position of solidarity and insight, but instead from a position of nervousness, or you work on auto-pilot.

In the event that you don't enjoy some time off, you might encounter burnout. It can leave you depleted, ineffective, and, surprisingly, discouraged.

Recap

Expanded times of stress can negatively affect your physical and mental prosperity. Enjoying some time off allows your cerebrum and body an opportunity to reset, reestablish, and adapt to the burdens of day-to-day existence.

Signs You Really want to Enjoy some time off

Once in a while, clearly, you want an excursion. In different cases, stress can surprise you. You may not be guaranteed to perceive when you're in danger of being overpowered and worn out.

Everybody answers stress in special ways. That implies that the indications of being overpowered are additionally profoundly personal. Nonetheless, there are a few general admonition signs that apply as a rule.

Assuming you're encountering at least one of the accompanying, begin arranging some personal time. This could mean a genuine excursion or even an end-of-the-week staycation to re-energize your batteries.

Key signs you want a break include:
- Changes in dietary patterns.
- Skepticism about work.
- Trouble concentrating.

- Becoming ill more often.
- Absence of energy.
- Absence of inspiration.
- Low mind-set.
- Dissatisfaction.
- Feeling unfocused or fluffy-headed.
- Actual side effects like cerebral pains or stomach aches.
- Horrible showing at work.
- Rest unsettling influences.
- Utilizing medications or liquor to adapt to stress.
- Pulling out from companions, family, or colleagues.

Try not to Hold on Until You're Worn Out

Try not to hold on until you've arrived at the mark of depletion to step back and enjoy some time off. Except if you as of now feel empowered, propelled, energized, imaginative, and completely drawn in working and in your connections, you'd probably profit from a get-away, on the grounds that it's smart to oversee stress before it feels overpowering.

Vacations, emotional health days, and normal taking care of oneself can keep you working at your best.

"I consider these breaks precaution care," says Rachel Goldman, PhD, FTOS, an authorized clinician having some expertise in wellness and health. The key is to keep ourselves from reaching the place where we totally need the break."

When to See a Specialist or Advisor

It's vital to take note that a significant number of these signs may likewise be side effects of an emotional health condition like wretchedness or uneasiness. Converse with your primary care physician or an emotional wellness proficient on the off chance that these side effects persevere even after you have some time off.

Advantages of Having some time off From Work

Excursions and, surprisingly, more limited breaks (like an evening off) where you get some physical and mental space from the requests of life can bring many prizes. A portion of the advantages you might appreciate when you have some time off include:

- **Diminished stress:** Clearly, you feel less stress when you're not in a distressing climate. Yet, breaks bring more than that. They intrude on the pattern of stress that can prompt being overpowered.

- **Rest:** By breaking out of the pattern of persistent stress, you can reestablish yourself truly and intellectually to a better spot.

- **More clear reasoning:** A constantly set-off stress reaction can prompt diminished inventiveness, memory issues, and different issues. So a break in the stress cycle can prompt more honed thinking and expanded imagination in all parts of your life.

- **Expanded efficiency:** All of this can improve you at your specific employment, more accessible in your connections, more vigorous with your family, and more ready to appreciate life after you return.

Recap

Having some time off not only allows you an opportunity to rest, but it can likewise advance more clear reasoning and more prominent efficiency.

Ways to enjoy some time off From Work

In the event that you really want a break, there are a few distinct choices for getting one. You can go for a long and lavish break, an unwinding and straightforward one, or something quick and painless. You could in fact have minutes-long breaks that you require over the course of the day to help efficiency and to hold back from feeling overpowered.

Vacation

A vacation is a genuine break, in the exemplary feeling of the word, and getting away is a higher priority than many individuals understand. That is the reason many vacation days go unused when they ought to be delighted without limit.

The way into a serene vacation is to focus on rest and fun when you go; don't overbook yourself with traveler exercises or carry such a lot of work with you that when you return, you believe you want an excursion from your excursion.

Many individuals feel having some time off adds an excess of work in planning to be away and afterward compensating for the missed time. While it might require a few exertions, the health and prosperity benefits you'll acquire than compensate for those expenses.

Staycation

The staycation is turning out to be increasingly famous, particularly as individuals have a more prominent need to enjoy some time off, however with less means to pull off a more extended trip. The staycation is about rest and unwinding, and getting a charge out of ah, back home again — a spot you are frequently excessively pushed and occupied to appreciate truly.

The way into a reviving staycation is equivalent to the way into a relaxing get-away, however, it very well may be fairly trickier to pull off: Don't get out of hand, and don't allow work to sneak in.

That implies no cleaning, office work, or managing customary obligations. You can either switch off the telephones, overlook email, and make it a highlight rest and play at home, or go to a close by lodging to make it more straightforward.

Playcation

Not many individuals discuss having a playcation, yet it's really smart: Remain at home, yet make it fun! The contrast between a staycation and a playcation is that staycations will quite often zero in more on resting and unwinding, while playcations are for — you've got it — fun!

With the difficult work and upsetting schedules that describe many individuals' ways of life, it's vital to have some good times as a method for re-energizing your batteries and be certain you're getting a charge out of life. You can give a few days to taking a playcation, or simply be certain you pepper in some fun consistently.

Brief Breaks

Once in a while you simply have to enjoy some time off from stress to the point of upsetting the stress reaction cycle, and afterward get once again into it. On the off chance that you simply need a break, get out for a bicycle ride, partake in a film, or even have a five-minute contemplation meeting.

Investing energy outside and active work can likewise be extraordinary stress relievers. Integrating these into your brief break, for example, taking a stroll outside around the block can assist you with getting all the more value for your money from your brief break.

Recap

Getaways can be an extraordinary method for enjoying some time off, yet you don't have to pass on town to loosen up. Staycations and playcations are perfect (and frequently more reasonable) choices, yet even short stretches where you go your brain and consideration regarding more soothing exercises can be valuable.

How This Affects You

Everybody needs a break occasionally to ease stress. Regardless of whether you can't take a major getaway, a staycation or brief break can be a significant method for feeling reestablished and revived. It is additionally crucial to enjoy short reprieves occasionally over the course of the day to re-energize your consideration and efficiency.

As frequently as conceivable Explain a few major problems

How long would it be a good idea for you to work prior to having some time off?

There are many variables that affect supported consideration, yet research recommends that the typical length that an individual can keep fixed on a solitary undertaking without encountering decreases in consideration or efficiency is around 30 to 45 minutes.

A recent report performed by the efficiency organization DeskTime found that the most useful individuals labor for 52 minutes and afterward require a 17-minute break. At the point when the review was rehashed seven years after the fact, the most useful individuals were laboring for 112 minutes prior to having some time off, an increment credited to changes in work life because of the Coronavirus pandemic.

A decent decision is that a brief break can assist you with remaining useful all through the work day.

How might you have some time off from work when you are discouraged?

Enjoying some time off when you are feeling discouraged is frequently difficult on the grounds that a considerable lot of the things that used to give you joy never again make a similar delight. One method for dealing with this is to spend your break periods participating in taking care of oneself exercises. Workouts, profound breathing, and contemplation might be useful for overseeing the side effects of sorrow.

Burning through 10 to 15 minutes on something like paying attention to music, writing in an appreciation diary, or partaking in some of your Tea are likewise extraordinary ways of having some time off and rehearsing taking care of oneself when you are feeling discouraged.

How would it be a good idea for you to respond when you are having some time off from work?

A break ought to be a genuine break from work — and that implies no browsing messages or other business-related obligations while you are on break. Figuring out how to revive your psyche and body can assist you with getting back to your errands with a reasonable brain, so getting up to extend or taking a stroll outside can be useful. So you can stop talking with colleagues. Research has found that laborers who associate at work are more joyful and better.

CHAPTER FIVE

Unwinding tips

The Excellence Of Slow Living: 12 Hints To Embrace A More Loosened up Way of Life

In the present quick-moving world, where everything moves dangerously fast, an ever-increasing number of individuals are going to the idea of "slow residing." However, the thing is slowly residing precisely.

Slow living is a direction for living that stresses dialing back, relishing each experience, and embracing a more careful and conscious way to deal with regular daily existence. It's tied in with living deliberately and being available in every second, as opposed to hurrying through existence without carving out the opportunity to encounter it.

The sluggish living development has its foundations in the sluggish food development, which started in Italy during the 1980s as a reaction to the cheap food culture that was dominating.

Slow food underscored the significance of neighborhood, practical, and occasional food, and the delight of imparting a feast to loved ones. This development long spread to different everyday issues and slow living was conceived.

How about we figure out how to begin slow living?

The Craft Of Slow Living: 12 Hints To Dial Back

1. Have a sluggish way to deal with your day-to-day existence.

In our bustling world, it tends to be not difficult to feel overpowered and depleted by the constant strain to keep up. The sluggish living development offers a reviving other option, supporting a less complex, more purposeful lifestyle.

By rethinking your needs, dialing back, and zeroing in on the things that really matter, you can develop a more noteworthy feeling of happiness and satisfaction in your day-to-day existence.

Embrace a slower surined, enjoy your everyday schedules, and relish the experiences that make life genuinely significant. With the sluggish carrying on with your way of life, you can discover a sense of reconciliation, happiness, and equilibrium in a world that frequently feels wild.

2. Be right now and live carefully.

One of the main sluggish living standards is this. In a world loaded with interruptions and mayhem, living with care and presence can appear to be a tricky objective.

In any case, developing this lifestyle by putting forth a cognizant attempt to zero in on the current moment is conceivable. By being completely present in every second, you can encounter a less difficult, seriously fulfilling, and less unpleasant life.

To break out of the pattern of bedlam and interruptions, many individuals go to care and reflection rehearses. These methods can assist you with figuring out how to zero in on the present and let go of stresses over the past or future.

By making a propensity for getting a kick out of the present time and place, you can start to embrace slow residing and work on your life.

Living with care and presence isn't tied in with overlooking the difficulties of life or keeping away from liabilities. Rather, it is tied in with moving toward your everyday undertakings and schedules with a more prominent feeling of mindfulness and expectation. By dialing back, being available, and zeroing in on the main thing, you can carry on with a more significant and satisfying life.

3. Remain associated with your local area.

It's not just about taking things at a slower surined - it's likewise about developing an association with your local area.

By chipping in, coordinating occasions, or essentially finding an opportunity to partake in the exercises accessible in your neighborhood, can foster significant associations with others and feel a more noteworthy feeling of harmony and satisfaction.

In a world that frequently underscores individual accomplishment and individual achievement, sluggish living development urges you to focus on connections and local area contribution. By zeroing in on the current second and being aware of the associations you make, you can encounter a more profound feeling of having a place and reason in your everyday existence.

So get some margin to dial back, engage locally, and relish the associations that give pleasure and importance to your life. By embracing the sluggish living way of thinking, you can make a seriously satisfying and fulfilling lifestyle.

4. Carry on with your existence with reason.

Carrying on with an intentional life is fundamental for your general joy and prosperity. By embracing your interests and focusing on self-awareness, you can discover a feeling of satisfaction and fulfillment in your everyday existence.

One method for developing design is through leisure activities or exceptional interests. These exercises give us joy and unwinding as well as add to our self-awareness and association with others.

Whether it's composition, painting, planting, or playing music, finding a leisure activity or exceptional interest can assist you with interfacing with your internal identity and tracking down significance in your life.

So set aside a few minutes for your number one exercises and interests, embrace the

*delight and reason they bring to your life,
and use them as a method for interfacing
with others and developing as a person.*

**5. Pursue consuming less and carrying
on with a moderate life.**

A sluggish carry-on with the way of life
embraces moderation and includes cleaning
up your home, working on your closet, and
diminishing your spending. This pattern
toward moderation is powered by the
acknowledgment that material belongings
don't liken to satisfaction or satisfaction.

*By turning into a moderate, you can lead an
obligation-free life, set aside cash, and
focus on spending on what you genuinely
need. Overconsumption likewise adds to
ecological issues, however, moderation*

offers an answer for diminishing waste and saving normal assets.

By consuming less, you can diminish your ecological effect and decidedly add to your general surroundings. Embrace an oversimplified mentality and moderate ways of behaving to help a sluggish person carry on with a way of life and carry on with a more significant life.

6. Make a guarantee to yourself that you'll dial back.

Many individuals trust that dialing back ought to be held for advanced age, however, there is a developing feeling that dialing back is fundamental at whatever stage in life.

Despite the fact that it very well may be challenging to dial back when life is occupied, it is critical to recall that time is restricted, and it's essential to consider how you need to spend it.

By focusing on a sluggish way of life, you can discover a lasting sense of reconciliation and satisfaction in the midst of the turmoil of life. Find an opportunity to ponder your choices and pick a day-to-day existence that lines up with your qualities. Embrace all that is genuine, and do whatever it takes not to let the turmoil of life upset your obligation to satisfaction, harmony, and quiet.

7. Esteem individuals you have in your life.

Might it be said that you are focusing intensely on individuals who make the biggest difference? Tragically, a considerable lot of us focus on innovation over our own connections. Incredibly, 90% of individuals really take a look at virtual entertainment during one-on-one discussions and 66% of individuals utilize their telephones during dinners.

We're residing in a general public where it's not difficult to convey online rather than face-to-face, prompting less credible connections.

While it's something extraordinary to grow your organization, it's critical to esteem face-to-face associations with individuals who share your qualities and interests. Make and keep up with space in your life for credible connections that engage you.

8. Practice slow living at work.

If you have any desire to rehearse a basic sluggish way of carrying on with your way of life, then you need to dismiss the quick-moving way of life that lauds hecticness without reason. A bustling timetable doesn't compare to a satisfying life nor does a surged day mean efficiency.

As a matter of fact, the consistent interruptions, gatherings, notices, and jabbering collaborators can obstruct one's concentration and capacity to deliver significant outcomes. The force of undistracted focus is obvious when one shows up before the expected time to the workplace and finishes days of work in only a couple of hours.

Embracing slow living at work involves focusing on assignments that lead to real results and disposing of pointless occupied work. Thus, you can think about the big picture before attacking the details, and live more deliberately.

9. Begin your days gradually and with a quiet psyche.

Beginning your day gradually is a pivotal part of slow living. Hurrying through your morning schedule establishes the vibe until the end of your day, leaving you feeling anxious, pushed, and zeroed in on scratching things off your rundown.

Then again, permitting yourself enough opportunity toward the beginning of the day can assist you with appreciating each experience and day-to-day schedule.

By dialing back in the first part of the day, you can carve out the opportunity to partake in your espresso or tea, appreciate your morning meal, and, surprisingly, sneak in some contemplation. This can assist you with feeling more present and focused over the course of the day, prompting expanded efficiency and a really satisfying day in general.

On the off chance that you're new to slow living, take a stab at beginning your day with a couple of additional minutes of calm time, a relaxed breakfast, or a stroll outside.

These little changes can have a major effect on your regular routine, assisting you with dialing back and partaking in the occasion.

10. Decline to participate in things that channel and exhaust you.

On the off chance that you are anticipating selecting slow living, it's essential to focus on your psychological and profound prosperity.

Saying "no" to things that channel you is a pivotal step towards that. It may very well be enticing to fill your timetable with fun and invigorating occasions, however, it's essential that your significant investments are restricted assets.

Figuring out how to say "no" to home bases, gatherings, and exercises that don't line up with your qualities or leave you feeling depleted is vital. It's OK to focus on alone time or serene exercises like perusing or going for a stroll in nature. By saying "no" to things that channel you, you make space for the things that really matter and give you pleasure.

Keep in mind, your significant investments are important. Safeguarding them is crucial for carrying on with a sluggish and deliberate life. In this way, whenever you're approached to go to an occasion or action that doesn't line up with your needs, make it a point to pleasantly decline.

11. Clean up your space and work on it.

Making a straightforward and coordinated living space can assist with working on your psychological clearness and decrease feelings of anxiety. Begin by cleaning up your living climate and disposing of pointless things, for example, garments you don't wear, and furniture that fills no need other than as a catch-for mess.

Doing so can assist with smoothing out your everyday schedule and make a more serene and useful air. A little change can hugely affect your general prosperity. So take a full breath, get out of the messiness, and partake in the advantages of an improved space.

12. Invest energy in nature and figure out your spot.

One of the most amazing at any point sluggish living tips is this one, and certainly one of the most misjudged.

In the quick-moving climate of a clamoring city, finding outside spaces where you can dial back and calmly inhale is fundamental for overseeing stress. Consider investigating parks, calm roads or parkways, libraries, exhibition halls, houses of prayer or chapels, graveyards, and greenhouses.

Every one of these areas gives a remarkable encounter, whether it's a tranquil green space in the city, a desert spring in the midst of the clamoring swarms, or a quiet setting encompassed by an old trees.

These spots offer a truly necessary escape from the rushed surge of city life and can give relief to help you unwind and re-energize. Despite the fact that they may not offer similar open doors for slow living as country regions, they actually give a significant break from the turmoil of city living.

Advantages Of Slow Living

Here are the absolute best advantages of the sluggish way of life;

- Diminishes stress and uneasiness levels.
- Energizes living right now and being careful.

- Further, develop rest quality and amount.
- Upgrades mental lucidity and concentration.
- Expands inventiveness and efficiency.
- Reinforces individual connections and social associations
- Advances in physical and close-to-homeprosperity.
- Lessons on ecological effect and carbon impression.
- Sets aside cash and lessens commercialization.
- Supports smart dieting propensities and home-cooking.
- Gives open doors to self-reflection and self-awareness.

- Cultivates a feeling of appreciation and appreciation for life's straightforward joy.
- Diminishes the requirement for performing various tasks and advances profound work.
- Energizes a more adjusted and feasible way of life.
- Assists with making a more profound association with nature and the general climate.

Slow living isn't simply a direction for living, but a cognizant choice to live deliberately and with reason. It is tied in with tracking down balance, focusing on the things that make the biggest difference, and working on your life to decrease stress and increment joy.

By setting aside some margin to dial back, you can partake in life's straightforward delights, center around self-awareness, and make significant associations with individuals and the world around you. Slow living offers various advantages that can work on your physical, mental, and close-to-homeprosperity.

Embracing a sluggish carrying on with a way of life might require a few changes, however, the prizes are certainly worth the work. So make a stride back, inhale profoundly, and partake in the excellence of slow living.

CHAPTER SIX

The Profound Stress of experiencing childhood in an unfortunate family might add to Obesity

As energy costs rise and the cost of most everyday items goes up, it is assessed that there are 4 million kids from more unfortunate families who have restricted or questionable admittance to quality food.

A recent report found that youngsters between the ages of eight and ten from homes that don't have simple admittance to quality food are multiple times bound to be stout contrasted with those from families that have sufficient food.

The review, which saw 50 moms and their infants, observed that kids in families where food shortage is an issue ate food when they were not ravenous and were bound to eat at least five snacks each day.

This is known as the "protection speculation" - the hypothesis is that individuals who don't have prepared admittance to food eat more to store energy when they do have food, to stay away from hunger in the future when food is scant.

Be that as it may, one more ongoing review directed at 394 grown-ups in the UK found no distinction in the absolute energy admission of food-shaky and food-secure individuals. What it found, however, was that the eating regimen of individuals without prepared admittance to good food was high in sugars, with less fiber and protein than others in the review.

The delays between when food-shaky individuals ate were likewise conflicting when contrasted with those with prepared admittance to quality food. This could be because of monetary reasons. Individuals who needed admittance to food couldn't keep standard spans between feasts, however rather ate as food opened up.

These exploration discoveries are concerning on the grounds that eating fatty food varieties (frequently high in sugar and fats and classed as undesirable food things) and skipping feasts have been viewed as connected with weight.

It proposes that eating rehearses that result from food uncertainty are factors that can prompt heftiness.

The job of stress

The profound cost of a youth living in destitution may likewise prompt corpulence. A 2018 examination survey of the elements prompting youth heftiness took a gander at the pretended by the family climate.

It proposes that low pay, the powerlessness to get to or bear the cost of nutritious food, and the stress brought about by the absence of pay and food establish a pessimistic mental and close-to-home climate for kids. This family disharmony disturbs homeostasis - the body's capacity to screen and keep up with its interior state.

Over the long run, this exploration proposes, this can prompt heftiness. One way this can happen is through indulging to adapt to stress- what is known as "close-to-homeeating" - when we use food to alleviate or encourage ourselves.

Expanded feelings of anxiety cause dysregulation of specific peptides and chemicals in the body, like insulin, cortisol, and ghrelin. Thus, more significant levels of these chemicals and peptides are related to expanded hunger for fatty food sources.

Youngsters are especially impacted on the grounds that they are currently creating propensities that will endure into adulthood. Gloomy feelings cause changes in pieces of the cerebrum that are answerable for the improvement of propensities and memory. In the event that kids eat solace food sources to decrease trouble and this turns into a propensity, they will utilize a similar methodology to answer future stress. Over the long haul, this could prompt heftiness.

close-to-homeeating

Other exploration studies have investigated the connection between profound eating and obesity. A review conducted in 2019 with 150 grown-ups investigated the connection between corpulence and financial drawbacks, mental trouble, and close-to-home eating.

It observed that lower financial status was related to higher pain and that higher trouble was related to more elevated levels of close-to-home eating. Thus, higher profound eating was related to higher body mass index.

Research done at the College of Salford with in excess of 600 grown-ups likewise observed that food frailty was related to a less fortunate eating regimen and that more prominent pain and eating to adapt was connected to higher body mass index.

This exploration was directed at grown-ups instead of taking a gander at the youth's reasons for corpulence. However, it recommends that mental misery and resulting profound eating is a pathway that joins neediness with heftiness.

Furthermore, a review done in the US with 676 youths from different foundations observed that apparent stress, stress, and confounded mindset were related with close to close-to-home eating.

In the UK, 29% of men and 27% of women are stout. This rate will be higher before very long in the event that more isn't finished to safeguard kids living in destitution.

What Are Normal Side Effects of Stress in Women?

Stress side effects in women can appear as both physical and mental issues, including anxiety, rest aggravations, and changes in feminine models.

Women might encounter stress uniquely in contrast to men because of a mix of organic, mental, and sociocultural elements. Hormonal variances, social and social jobs, and natural weaknesses can impact these reactions.

It's critical to know about how stress can appear in your body and to go to proactive lengths to lighten these impacts.

What are the normal side effects of stress in a woman?

Side effects differ from one individual to another, however, a few commonplace signs and side effects of stress in women might include:

Profound side effects

- Expanded nervousness or stress.
- Feeling overpowered.
- Mind-set swings.
- Crabbiness or outrage.
- Bitterness or despondency.
- Diminished sex drive.

Mental side effects:

- Hustling considerations.
- Trouble concentrating.
- Distraction.
- Trouble deciding.

- Negative or dreary reasoning.

Actual side effects

- Muscle strain and cerebral pains.
- Weariness and low energy.
- Rest aggravations (a sleeping disorder).
- Changes in hunger (gorging or loss of craving)
- Stomach-related issues (e.g., stomachaches or sickness).
- Debilitated invulnerable framework, prompting more regular ailments.
- Expanded pulse.
- Feminine anomalies.
- Skin issues (e.g., skin inflammation or dermatitis).
- Ripeness issues.

Do people answer stress in an unexpected way?

Indeed, people will generally answer stress in an unexpected way, both regarding their physiological and social reactions. These distinctions in sexual orientation are impacted by a mix of organic, hormonal, and cultural variables.

As per the American Psychological Association (APA), here are a portion of the vital contrasts among women and men:

Impression of stress influence: Around 88% of women and 78% of men accept that stressfirmly affects an individual's well-being.

Significance of overseeing stress: 68% of women and just 52% of men consider overseeing stress Exceptionally/critically.

Communicating concern: 25% of women and 17% of men recognize that they're not doing what's necessary with regard to overseeing stress.

Activity to lessen stress: Around 70% of women and around half of men report attempting to diminish worry about the beyond 5 years.

Stress the management'smethodologies: women utilize different stress board techniques, including perusing (51%), investing energy with family or companions (44%), supplicating (41%), going to strict administrations (24%), shopping (18%), getting a back rub or visiting a spa (14%), and seeing a psychological wellness proficient (5%). Men are more disposed to be involved in playing sports as a stress board procedure (14%).

Faith in proficient assistance: women have areas of strength for the viability of clinicians in assisting with way of life and conduct changes and adapting to persistent sicknesses, while men have a more vulnerable confidence in their viability.

A recent report conducted in southern Italy analyzed feelings of anxiety during the progress from joblessness to work in 395 members (62% men, 38% women). Most had typical to low feelings of anxiety, however when isolated by sex, women (22.7%) revealed higher stress Than men (11%).

How in all actuality does it influence the female body?

While all kinds of people can be actually impacted by stress, women may at times encounter exceptional physiological reactions to stressors.

Here are a few different ways stress can influence the female body:

- **Feminine abnormalities:** Persistent stress can prompt unpredictable monthly cycles, missed periods, or more extreme Premenstrual Syndrome (PMS) side effects. In an investigation of youthful female health science understudies, there were major areas of strength between high feelings of anxiety and feminine issues, like amenorrhea and premenstrual disorder.
- **Ripeness issues:** Higher feelings of anxiety have been related to

troubles in getting pregnant. The stress of attempting to imagine can likewise compound the issue. Research recommends that tending to mental misery with mediation might further develop fruitful results for women attempting to get pregnant.

- **Hormonal changes:** stress can upset the hormonal equilibrium, which might influence mindset and generally speaking well-being. One study discovered that stress during the early monthly cycle stage prompted expanded progesterone and cortisol levels.

- **Expanded torment awareness:** stress can bring down torment resilience, making women more helpless to conditions like stress migraines, headache assaults, and ongoing agony. Research demonstrates that women for the most part show a higher aversion to torment than men, announcing lower torment limits, resiliencia, and more noteworthy agony power in trial settings.

How might women better oversee stress?

women can more readily oversee through different systems:

- **Normal activity:** Actual work decreases stress chemicals and advances the arrival of endorphins, which are regular state-of-mind lifters.

- **Sound eating regimen:** Eating a decent eating routine rich in natural products, vegetables, entire grains, and incline proteins can uphold general prosperity and stress management.

- **Satisfactory rest:** Focus on great rest cleanliness by keeping a reliable rest plan and making a serene sleep time schedule.

- **Care and unwinding:** Procedures like contemplation, profound breathing activities, and moderate muscle unwinding can assist with lessening stress.

- **Social help:** Interface with companions, friends, and family, as friendly connections can offer profound help during distressing times. Research with youthful grown-ups proposes that social help can be a huge defensive variable for emotional wellness, especially among young women.

- **Hobbies and interests:** Take part in exercises you appreciate to ease stress and advance a feeling of satisfaction.

- **Practice appreciation:** Keep an appreciation diary to zero in on certain parts of life and decrease harping on stressors.

Main concern

Assuming you're a lady managing stress, it's critical to perceive that it can influence you truly, inwardly, and typically. Watch for side effects like weakness, touchiness, feminine abnormalities, and stress.

Stress can hurt both your psychological and actual well-being, so feel free to help and practice taking care of yourself to really oversee it.

Treatments That Work for Stress

Stress is a typical piece of life — great stress and terrible stress. With terrible stress, you have both physical and close-to-homeresponses to specific triggers that can make you stress and feel tense. Stress can vacillate at work or at home, while testing circumstances and different changes in your day-to-day existence can set off it, as well.

On the off chance that you're interested in how you can oversee stress through treatment, read on to look further into what sorts of treatments and specialists can help.

What treatments work for stress?

While stress itself is a typical piece of life, repeating stress that impedes your everyday exercises and general prosperity isn't. Stress can show itself in various ways, including unnecessary stress, failure to rest around evening time, and body hurts.

Stress can incur significant damage, however, treatment can assist you with overseeing it better. A few sorts of treatment might try and furnish you with techniques to adapt to future stress. The following are the most generally involved treatments for stress and related psychological health conditions.

Mental conduct treatment (MCT) for transient assistance

MCT is maybe one of the most widely recognized sorts of treatment that anyone could hope to find, as it tends to your thinking examples and ways of behaving. Your specialist will assist you with recognizing your stressors, and assist you with concocting better reactions to lessen the effect of your triggers.

MCT might be utilized on either a present moment or a long-haul premise. This can make it reasonable to assist with treating persistent emotional wellness conditions, as well as assisting you with overcoming horrible mishaps and different reasons for intense stress.

You might profit from MCT in the event that you're worried about:

- Nervousness.
- Misery.
- Bipolar turmoil.
- Rest problems, like a sleeping disorder.
- Fears.
- Fanatical impulsive issue.

Psychodynamic treatment

Like MCT, psychodynamic treatment intends to assist you with recognizing figured designs that might directly conduct reactions. Psychodynamic treatment, be that as it may, is utilized on an all the more long-haul premise. It could be the most ideal for stress brought about by well-established issues that you have been managing, which are interwoven with other emotional wellness conditions, like uneasiness and misery.

Social treatment

Social treatment is like MCT with its attention on changes in conduct. However, dissimilar to MCT, conduct treatment is more centered around your activities, instead of your viewpoints.

As indicated by this kind of treatment, your activities are directed by past ways of behaving. By changing your conduct reactions to stretch now, you can make new examples and conceivably keep away from additional stress.

Conduct treatment will in general turn out best for long-haul triggers of stress, including horrible mishaps, as well as conditions like uneasiness, fears, and consideration shortage hyperactivity jumble.

Openness treatment

Openness treatment is a procedure customarily used to treat fears, PTSD, and nervousness problems. You could profit from this kind of treatment on the off chance that you have a psychological wellness condition that makes you keep away from specific circumstances, items, individuals, and spots.

This sort of treatment may likewise assist with tending to ongoing stress assuming that you practice evasion with an end goal to stay away from more stress. Sadly, such aversion can exacerbate stress causing you to feel much more uncomfortable.

Openness treatment works by permitting your specialist to help steadily open you to the triggers that you deliberately stay away from. That's what the thought is, over the long run, you will become acquainted with these apprehensions and become less worried about them.

Bunch treatment

At times, bunch treatment might be a choice assuming you're managing an incredibly upsetting occasion. Models incorporate a catastrophic event, kid misfortune, and separation, and the sky's the limit from there. A prepared specialist drives meetings, and you might find the social environment permits you to feel engaged and less alone.

What sort of advisor is best for stress?

Prepared analysts or psychotherapists are by and large the best sort of psychological wellness experts for stress-related treatments. Their central goal is to assist you with distinguishing triggers of stress while cooperatively fostering an arrangement with you to oversee them. Psychotherapists are additionally alluded to as "talk specialists."

While searching for an advisor, you can ask an imminent expert what modalities they work in. For instance, many talk advisors use MCT, while others could have practical experience in psychodynamic treatment. Likewise, a few psychotherapists spend significant time in stress and related emotional wellness conditions like uneasiness.

While analysts and psychotherapists will generally be the most supportive in helping their clients with conduct changes in light of stress, a few circumstances might warrant different sorts of emotional health experts who likewise use talk treatment strategies. These include:

- **Therapists,** who can likewise regulate psychological health meds and have clinical preparation.

- **Bunch guide,** who has some expertise in working with a little gathering with comparative battles

- **Play advisors** for more youthful youngsters

- **School guides,** who might address the stress of school-matured kids, as well as understudies.

What else assists with stress?

Besides treatment, there are different advances you can take to decrease stress in your day-to-day existence at this moment. You can begin with the following:

- **Work-out consistently.** Research shows that in any event, strolling for 30 minutes every day can diminish stress and lift your general state of mind.

- **Plan normal unwinding spans.** Accomplish something that loosens up you for basically a few minutes every day. Simply a few thoughts incorporate washing up, delicate yoga extends, profound breathing activities, or perusing a book.

- **Forestall social disengagement.** While seeing loved ones for in-person exercises can help, in any event, settling on telephone decisions or talking practically can keep you socially associated and lessen your stress.

- **Rethink your needs.** Center around everyday undertakings without stressing a lot over what you can't finish. Likewise, say "no" to pointless errands, and agent additional work when you begin to feel overpowered.

The above strategies can work for both ongoing and intense types of stress, and they can supplement any treatments you choose to attempt. On the off chance that you're battling with continuous stress, see a psychological wellness proficient for exhortation.

The Action Item

Periodic stress isn't really a reason to worry on the off chance that you can oversee it all alone. However, on the off chance that stress slows down your life consistently and you're feeling overpowered, it might very well be an ideal opportunity to look for help.

Left untreated, progressing (ongoing) stress might add to (or deteriorate) certain psychological wellness conditions, including tension, post-traumatic stress disorder (PTSD), and discouragement.

Unmanaged stress can likewise have different outcomes for your well-being. These may incorporate stomach-related illnesses, hypertension (hypertension), and rest problems. Long-haul stress is likewise connected to metabolic problems.

Treatment can be a priceless instrument for stress, whether you're going through a surprisingly difficult stretch or on the other hand assuming that you've been battling with persistent stress. It might actually address stress connected with psychological wellness conditions or ongoing diseases.

What is a Concern Diary for stress?

What do you do when you feel anxious or stressed? Do you vent to any individual who will tune in? Or on the other hand, do you serenely write down your viewpoints in a diary?

For some individuals, the response is most likely the previous — and that checks out.

For some purposes, venting might prompt a soothing arrival of feelings.

In any case, utilizing a diary to write down your burdens and stresses can be a powerful device to assist you with inclining toward awkward feelings. It can likewise assist you with analyzing what you're feeling and give you a way ahead.

As somebody who has frequently been portrayed as a "conceived worrier," I realize quite well the way that weakening concern can be.

Stress can take care of sensations of uneasiness, stress, and dread. It can prompt catastrophizing. I can overthink even the most apparently direct situation and work myself into a frenzy.

A well-qualified assessment

As per Dublin-based advocate and psychotherapist Fiona Lobby, it's normal for stresses to seem greater in our minds than they are in actuality.

They can all start empowering each other, merging and making our sensations of nervousness rise,". "Recording concerns and stresses engages us to obtain a perspective over what are confirmed concerns and speculative worries."

As well as giving a point of view, journaling can assist us with being more mindful of how we're deciphering things.

"It can assist us with handling our concerns so we can turn out to be more mindful of the distinction between the occasion and our understanding of the occasion," says Lobby.

What Are the Social Side Effects of Stress?

Leveling up your stress the management's abilities can assist with working on normal conduct side effects of stress nail gnawing, skin picking, and gorging.

Stress happens when your body answers a test. It may very well be from controlled boosts, such as lifting a significant burden, or it can happen in light of genuine or seen dangers.

Your stress reaction is there to assist you with dealing with the test within reach. Temporarily, it provides you with a required increase in energy and readiness. stress that sticks around excessively lengthy, notwithstanding, and becomes rehashed or ongoing, can begin to wear you out.

While you're feeling worried, worried, or stressed, you might begin to see the side effects of delayed stress. Since social side effects of stress are outside, they're often the ones perceived first.

What are the sorts of responses to push?

Stress can influence everybody remarkably. Two individuals in a similar definite circumstance of stress might have very various responses.

As per Michelle English, an authorized clinical social specialist from San Diego, California, stress responses ordinarily fall into four classes:

- **Physical:** encounters like migraines, muscle stress, and weariness.
- **Close to home:** steady sensations of uneasiness, stress, outrage, and misery.
- **Mental:** unfortunate focus, memory changes, and learning impedance.
- **Conduct:** social withdrawal, indulging, hair spinning, and substance abuse.

Inside these, the lines aren't clear 100% of the time. You can have a conduct response, for instance, that is additionally personal, such as raging at a friend or family member during a discussion.

"Irregularly, people don't see that the physical, up close and personal, and lead changes they are experiencing are a response to push," explains English. "It tends to be simple for somebody to misattribute their responses to something different or disregard them through and through."

Instances of Social Side Effects of Stress

Social side effects of stress can be precarious to recognize. They might be unpretentious, such as picking at the skin around your fingers, or they can be more self-evident, such as going on a shopping binge.

As per the Stress in America 2020 report, almost 50% of all grown-ups report that stress negatively influences their conduct here and there.

Models include:

- Nail gnawing.
- Skin picking.
- Lip biting.
- Hair whirling/pulling.
- Pacing.
- Squirming.
- Foot tapping.
- Gorging.
- Teeth crushing/holding.
- Unreasonable dozing/a sleeping disorder.
- Fast discourse.
- Factiousness.
- Smoking.
- Drinking liquor.
- Substance abuse.
- Perilous sexual commitment.
- Social withdrawal.
- Diminished working out.

- Expanded ways of managing money.
- Dismissing individual consideration.
- Betting.

What causes the side effects of stress?

Social side effects of stress differ generally, and everything from your hereditary qualities to your character type can be compelling.

Correspondingly as we gain genuine attributes, our characteristics can similarly make us more powerless to experience expanded responses," checks out to Dr. Raffaello Antonino, a guiding therapist and senior instructor at London Metropolitan College, London, Britain.

"A few people could have hereditary cosmetics that make them more receptive to stretching, impacting their cerebrum science and hormonal vacillations."

Notwithstanding hereditary qualities, Antonino shows social Streetside effects are affected by:

Individual history and previous encounters
Encountering injury, misuse, or disregard, may make you become more delicate to future stressors.

Current strategies for dealing with especially difficult times

Individuals who can defy stress head-on, says Antonino, may disperse their belongings all the more immediately contrasted with the people who default to evasion survival techniques.

Accessible emotionally supportive networks

The more emotionally supportive networks you have, the more uncertain you might be about allowing stress to move toward the place of conduct.

Climate and way of life

"Constant work stress, undesirable ways of life, or being in a reliably regrettable climate can enhance stress reactions," says Antonino.

Social and cultural standards

Social assumptions and marks of disgrace can influence whether stress is assimilated, bringing about more profound and mental trouble, or externalized into additional conduct side effects.

Character type

"Certain character types, similar to fussbudgets or those with high neuroticism, might be more inclined to show extraordinary social responses to stretch," Antonino states. "Running against the norm, those with a normally hopeful or tough demeanor could display less outward signs."

Ways to oversee Street side effects

Social side effects of stress can be overseen in a considerable lot of the same ways as different side effects of stress.

Building support

Making and remaining mindful of associations with predictable individuals in your ordinary presence can assist you with causing serious strong regions for a construction that will be there when difficulties are insane.

At the point when you have working emotionally supportive networks, you're ready to facilitate the weight of stress through sharing and associating with others.

Growing new adapting choices

English likewise prescribes developing elective ways of adapting to stress. This incorporates participating in actual activity, nature openness, or taking part in side interests or artworks when you want to assuage some stress.

Antonino adds that rehearsing care can be a method for making a space between stressors and your response to them, giving a valuable chance to pick a more gainful reaction.

Laying out limits

Defining clear limits for you and the people around you can assist with restricting how frequently you're placed in circumstances that vibe overpowering and distressing.

Way of life changes

Eating a reasonable eating regimen, practicing routinely, and getting a lot of rest can assist with diminishing the effect of stress.

Other valuable way of life changes incorporate restricting liquor utilization, smoking, and wiping out substance use.

Looking for proficient direction

It's alright to look for help for overseeing stress. Emotional wellness experts are there to assist you with creating adapting abilities and address the hidden reasons for stress.

"… mental remaking techniques, for instance, reconsidering your considerations or testing pessimistic reasoning can assist you with dealing with close-to-home responses and ways of behaving related to stress," English says.

Main concern

Social side effects of stress are your outside reactions while adapting to testing circumstances. Hair spinning, nail gnawing, squirming, and skin picking are unpretentious models.

Not every person encounters social side effects while managing stress. Hereditary qualities, individual history, current survival strategies, and your encouraging groups of people can all assume a part in the sort of side effects you experience.

Like other stress responses, conduct side effects of stress can be overseen through way of life changes, development of new survival techniques, and looking for proficient assistance when fundamental.

Mental stress

Outline

Stress. It's a six-letter word that a significant number of us fear. Whether it's a strained connection with a chief or tension from loved ones, we as a whole face upsetting circumstances every now and then.

For a few of us, these occasions happen irregularly. For other people, day-to-day life is an ordinary piece of life.

Mental stress definition

There's a decent opportunity we can all recognize negative stress, yet do you have any idea that stress can likewise be positive?

Great stress, called eustress, can really be gainful to you. In contrast to terrible stress, or misery, great stress can assist with inspiration, concentration, energy, and execution. For certain individuals, it can likewise feel invigorating.

Then again, terrible stress regularly causes tension, concern, and a diminishing in exhibition. It additionally feels awkward, and it can prompt more difficult issues on the off chance that not tended to.

Mental stress impacts

Stress can adversely affect our lives. It can cause states of being, like cerebral pains, stomach-related issues, and rest aggravations. It can likewise cause mental and close-to-homestrains, including disarray, nervousness, and melancholy.

As per the American Mental Association, untreated ongoing stress, or stress that is consistent and endures over a drawn-out timeframe, can bring about hypertension or a debilitated safe framework.

It can likewise add to the improvement of corpulence and coronary illness.

Mental stress signs

There's a differentiation between a stressor and real stress. A complaint can be an individual, spot, or circumstance that is causing you stress. Stress is the genuine reaction to one or a mix of those stressors.

There are quite a few circumstances that can cause stress. Dr. Gary Brown, an authorized psychotherapist, expresses a portion of the more normal stressors include:

- Relationships clash at home.
- New or expanding work liabilities.

- Expanding requests.

- Monetary strain.

- Loss of a friend or family member.

- Medical conditions.

- Moving to another area.

openness to at least one horrible episode, like a fender bender or a vicious wrongdoing Knowing how to detect the indications of stress is the first move toward quite a while to deal with its unfriendly impacts.

A portion of the more normal physical, mental, and close-to-homeindications of constant stress include:

- Quick pulse.

- Raised pulse.

- Feeling overpowered.

- Exhaustion.

- Trouble dozing.

- Unfortunate critical thinking.
- Dread that the stressor will not disappear.
- Diligent considerations around at least one stressor.
- Changes in conduct, including so.

Ways of Overseeing Stress

With regards to overseeing stress, simplifying changes can go far in working on your general health and diminishing stress. Having devices and techniques you can go to in unpleasant circumstances can forestall your feelings of anxiety from rising.

Track down an equilibrium

It's critical to structure a portion of your time so you can be serenely occupied without being overpowered, Earthy colored says.

"Really buckling down doesn't ordinarily like working productively," he said. Working a lot can decrease efficiency, truth be told.

Be caring to yourself

Understanding that you're not feeble on the grounds that you're feeling stress is significant, Earthy colored says. stress is an exceptionally typical response to the stressors in your day-to-day existence.

Rest on individuals you trust

Before your feelings of anxiety heighten, contact somebody you trust, like a companion, relative, or collaborator. Talking about your thoughts or venting your interests might assist with diminishing your stress.

Keep a diary

Put away the opportunity to ponder your day. Record any considerations or sentiments you're having. This can be a valuable instrument to assist you with better comprehension of your stressors and how you respond to stress, Earthy colored says.

Eat even, ordinary dinners

With regards to overseeing stress, appropriate nourishment is your companion. Skipping feasts can bring down your glucose, which can push down your state of mind. At times, this can likewise set off extreme sensations of outrage and disappointment, Earthy colored says.

Work-out routinely

Taking part in customary active work can work on your general health and decrease your feelings of anxiety. At the point when you work out, your body discharges endorphins. These vibe great chemicals can likewise ease the side effects of melancholy and nervousness.

Get a lot of rest

Your capacity to oversee stress diminishes when you're worn out. Attempt to get a prescribed seven to nine hours every evening. On the off chance that you have sleep deprivation, expect to get as much rest as possible, then form in times of rest during the day.

Practice unwinding works out

These activities, which can incorporate profound, slow breathing and moderate muscle unwinding, include straining and afterward loosening up different gatherings of muscles.

Attempt to cut out three minutes, three times each day to rehearse these activities, says Dr. Russell Morfitt, a clinician.

Plan your concern

While it might feel abnormal from the beginning, consider booking the concern to explicit pieces of the day, Morfitt says. "Right when we slant toward our sensations of fear by intentionally looking throughout our stressors and not avoiding them or moving away from them, they every now and again lose their power," he said.

Working with an expert

A specialist or emotional wellness expert can likewise assist you with tracking down ways of dealing with your stress.

Think about working with emotional health proficiency in the event that your stress is ongoing or joined by day-to-day migraines, tight jaw, fibromyalgia, or consistent exhaustion, says Dr. David J. Puder of Loma Linda College Social Medication Place.

You ought to likewise see psychological health proficient in the event that you have sensations of wretchedness, self-destructive contemplations, and fits of anxiety.

While searching for a psychological wellness proficient, ask companions or relatives for references. After your most memorable meeting, Puder says to ponder the accompanying inquiries:

- Will you trust the advisor?

- Do you feel appreciated and got it?

- Do you feel good to shout out in the event that you contradict them?

- Might you at any point see that they care about you as a person?

Do Stress Balls Work?

Stress balls can be a useful device for overseeing transitory stress and strain by giving a material interruption and advancing unwinding.

Stress balls are delicate, malleable, and simple to-press objects intended to give an actual outlet to stress, strain, and anxious energy.

The material experience and monotonous crushing of stress can offer a mitigating tactile interruption that really diverts your consideration away from tension. For some individuals, they're a reasonable and easy-to-utilize instrument for overseeing brief episodes of stress.

Are stress balls compelling?

The viability of stress balls fluctuates among people and relies upon the particular circumstance and the hidden reasons for stressor nervousness. While some might find them valuable for gentle stress, research on their adequacy is blended.

One review examined the effect of utilizing a stress ball as an interruption strategy on stress, important bodily functions, and solace levels in hemodialysis patients. The exploration affected 45 individuals, with one gathering utilizing a stress ball during dialysis meetings.

While there were no massive changes in fundamental signs or solace levels, the stress ball diminished stress in the gathering that pre-owned it.

One more study discovered that stress balls utilized during lithotripsy techniques for kidney or ureter stones were found to decidedly affect decreasing agony levels in patients.

Nonetheless, they didn't fundamentally influence uneasiness levels during the methodology. Further examination is expected to more readily comprehend the adequacy of stress balls in overseeing agony and nervousness in this unique situation.

Could stress assist with tension?

Stress balls might be useful for uneasiness now and again. They give you something material to zero in on and can assist you with unwinding by pressing and delivering. However, remember that they turn out contrastingly for everybody and are typically better for gentle nervousness.

Stress balls might give impermanent help from situational (state) tension by offering a tactile interruption. For long-haul general (characteristic) uneasiness, they can be essential for a more extensive unwinding procedure yet may not be the sole arrangement.

What are the advantages of crushing a stress ball?

Crushing a stress ball can offer a few expected benefits, including:

- **Stress decrease:** stress balls might assist with diminishing stress and strain by giving an actual outlet to apprehensive energy.
- **Unwinding:** The redundant pressing and delivering movement might advance unwinding and a feeling of quiet.
- **Further developed center:** Utilizing a stress ball might assist with further developing fixation and concentration, especially during upsetting or restless minutes.
- **Material interruption:** It gives material and tangible interruption that can redirect consideration from nervousness inciting contemplations or circumstances.

- **Hand strength:** Standard utilization of stress balls can assist with reinforcing hand and lower arm muscles, which might be useful for joint pain or as a feature of exercise-based recuperation.
- **Care:** Crushing a stress ball can act as a type of care work, assisting you with remaining grounded right now.
- **Compact stress help:** stress balls are small and versatile, making them a helpful in-a-hurry device for stress help.

Step-by-step instructions to utilize a stress ball

To utilize a stress ball, hold it in one hand and crush it immovably, then discharge.

Rehash this pressing and delivering movement to assist with lessening stress and strain. You can utilize it while sitting, standing, or during snapshots of stress or tension for unwinding.

How long would it be a good idea for you to crush a stress ball?

Press the stress ball however long it actually decreases stress and strain. Certain individuals might find it supportive to press and deliver the stress ball for a couple of moments, while others could involve it for a few minutes. There's no severe time limit, so use it as an instrument for unwinding and stress help that turns out best for you.

What are the constraints of a stress ball?

While stress balls can be useful for stress help and unwinding, they have their cutoff points and may not address all parts of stressor tension. Here are a few constraints and things stress balls commonly don't do:

- **Complex stressors:** stress balls may not successfully address mind-boggling or multi-layered wellsprings of stress, for example, business-related stressor relationship issues.

- **Serious uneasiness issues:** In the event that you have tension problems like summed up nervousness confusion or frenzy problems, stress balls alone are probably not going to give adequate alleviation.

- **Long haul stress the management:** While they can give fleeting help, stress balls are definitely not an extensive answer for long haul stress on the board. Viable stress the board frequently requires a blend of methodologies, including treatment, exercise, and way of life measures.

Main concern

Stress balls are flexible articles intended for pressing and control. They can give a basic, helpful method for easing fleeting stress and strain through material interruption.

Stress balls can be a helpful instrument however are best when joined with different methods, particularly for tending to complicated or long-haul stressors.

Light to Direct Drinking Might Assist with easing stress, Help Your Heart

Scientists find moderate drinking might assist with easing stress.

The study could make sense of past examinations tracking down better health results for light-to-direct consumers.

Analysts analyzed information on in excess of 50,000 individuals signed up for the Mass General Brigham Biobank.

Light to direct liquor utilization might bring down the gamble of cardiovascular occasions, for example, coronary failure and stroke by diminishing movement in pieces of the mind that answer stress, new examination claims.

Yet, scientists alert that liquor additionally conveys health chances.

"We are not supporting the utilization of liquor to decrease the gamble of coronary failures or strokes, due to other concerning impacts of liquor on wellbeing," concentrate on creator Dr. Ahmed Tawakol, a cardiologist and co-head of the Cardiovascular Imaging Exploration Center at Massachusetts General Medical clinic in Boston, said in a news discharge.

All things considered, scientists needed to comprehend how light direct liquor utilization (one to two beverages per day for men and one beverage daily for women) diminishes cardiovascular illness, as seen in other research.

"In the event that we could find the component, the objective is to find different methodologies that could reproduce or prompt liquor's defensive heart impacts without the unfriendly effects of liquor," said Tawakol.

"On the off chance that we could find the instrument, the objective is to find different methodologies that could reproduce or initiate liquor's defensive cardiovascular impacts without the antagonistic effects of liquor," said Tawakol.

Decreased stress signals in the mind

In this observational review, specialists analyzed information on in excess of 50,000 individuals signed up for the Mass General Brigham Biobank.

Individuals finished up an overview at the hour of enlistment, which incorporated an inquiry concerning their liquor utilization during the earlier year.

Specialists acquired data from members' clinical records about any major cardiovascular occasions they encountered during the review time frame. This included coronary episodes, stroke, fringe vascular sickness, and cardiovascular breakdown.

They found that light-to-direct consumers had a lower hazard of major cardiovascular occasions, considering the hereditary, clinical, way of life, and financial variables.

Then, specialists concentrated on a subset of around 750 individuals who had recently gone through cerebrum imaging for clinical reasons not connected with the review.

Light-to-direct consumers had lower action in the amygdala — a district of the cerebrum engaged with stress flagging — contrasted with individuals who drank practically no liquor.

Individuals with lower stress signals in the amygdala likewise had fewer major cardiovascular occasions, the outcomes showed.

"We found that the mind changes in light to direct consumers made sense as a critical part of the defensive cardiovascular impacts," said Tawakol.

Individuals with tension helped more

Other exploration has found that liquor diminishes how responsive the amygdala is to compromising improvements, like unfortunate and irate countenances.

The new review, however, is quick to show that this hosing of action in the amygdala in light of liquor might decidedly affect the cardiovascular framework, the scientists said.

"At the point when the amygdala is too ready and cautious, the thoughtful sensory system is elevated, which drives up pulse and increments pulse, and triggers the arrival of incendiary cells," said Tawakol.

"In the event that the stress is ongoing, the outcome is hypertension, expanded irritation, and a significant gamble of weight, diabetes and cardiovascular illness," he added.

Specialists likewise tracked down that inside the whole gathering of members, light to direct drinking was connected to more noteworthy reductions in major cardiovascular occasions for individuals with a background marked by tension, contrasted with others.

Albeit light to direct consumers saw a diminishing in their gamble for cardiovascular sickness, they likewise had a higher gamble of disease.

Likewise, drinking higher measures of liquor — in excess of 14 beverages per week — was related to diminished by and large mind action, which the analysts said might be connected to unfriendly mental well-being.

Another examination has shown that being weighty or hitting the bottle hard can adversely affect well-being, like expanding the gamble of kicking the bucket for any reason and from malignant growth explicitly.

The creators of the review presume that the outcomes could guide the way to new medications that lessen stress signals in the cerebrum, without the adverse consequences of liquor.

Scientists are presently concentrating on whether work out, stress-decrease treatments like contemplation, and prescriptions can house these stress-related signals and potentially lead to cardiovascular advantages.

Solid ways of managing stress

Gregory Jantz, Ph., the organizer behind The Middle, A Position of Trust in Edmonds, Wash., an office for the therapy of misery, said constant stress turned into an issue for a great many Americans during the Coronavirus pandemic.

In the American Mental Association's "Stress in America 2022" overview, almost a fourth of individuals said that most days they are so worried they can't work.

Around the world, the pandemic set off a 25% ascent in despondency and tension, as per the World Health Organization.

Jantz, creator of "The Uneasiness Reset: A Groundbreaking Way to Deal with Beating Dread, stress, stress, Fits of anxiety, OCD and that's just the beginning," said even today, nervousness stays a gigantic issue in the US, with some unsettling impacts.

"We discovered that people have been using food, drink, and marijuana. We've likewise seen an immense expansion in addictions and habit-forming conduct," he said

Do whatever it takes not to drink to "bring some alleviation"

While certain individuals might drink liquor to de-stress — to "offer some relief" — Jantz said when you are anxious, having only one drink is troublesome.

All things considered, he proposes making a couple of way of life changes like eating a solid eating routine, drinking water rather than liquor (or sweet beverages), and adding greater development to your day.

"Every one of those are truly basic, solid activities," he said. "In any case, they're things that during the pandemic, individuals quit doing."

Moreover, Jantz said it tends to be useful to recognize triggers for uneasiness in your life, like virtual entertainment or every minute of everyday consistent pattern of media reporting.

In the event that these are causing you stress, "you must change your place of concentration," he said, specifically moving your consideration regarding sound associations with loved ones.

We should have those positive people in our lives, no matter what's going on around us in the world," he said. "I'm not saying overlook the unpleasant things, but rather they can't be your place of concentration."

On the off chance that you keep on encountering nervousness that influences your day-to-day exercises, or is turning out to be more regrettable, look for help from a specialist or emotional health proficient.

Do My Feelings of Anxiety Influence the Protein Levels in My Urine?

It's not unexpected to have a little protein in your urine, however high fixations can be an indication of a more serious hidden condition.

The human body is astonishing. Alongside dealing with an enormous number of cycles and frameworks naturally, it likewise knows how to caution us when something is off-base.

Like how the variety and consistency of your nasal bodily fluid can show disease, your urine can likewise be an early sign that things aren't as one.

The vast majority know that the shade of our urine can be a simple method for deciding if an individual is appropriately hydrated. Moreover, for some individuals, a urine test is the most important phase in finding a pregnancy. Notwithstanding, different substances can likewise be found in the urine in any event, when they ought not to be there — or in huge focuses.

Assuming you figure out that you have protein in your urine, you could keep thinking about whether you ought to be stressed. This article will assist you with understanding having protein in your urine, how it arrives, and whether it's risky.

Short response: Can stress cause protein in the urine?

While stress can in some cases be a reason for transient proteinuria, it's not connected with long-haul types of the condition.

All things considered, individuals with protein in their urine for stretched-out periods are bound to encounter more serious medical issues like kidney illness or a family background of, diabetes, and hypertension.

Having a limited quantity of protein in your urine is typical. In any case, in high focus, it can in some cases be an indication of kidney harm. At the point when you have high convergences of protein in your urine, it's a condition called proteinuria.

Will stress cause protein in the urine during pregnancy?

Pregnancy and toxemia (a sort of hypertension related to pregnancy) are both associated with dependable proteinuria. Notwithstanding, an expansion in protein present in the urine is ordinary, even in a predictable pregnancy.

The typical urinary protein range for a pregnancy in the third trimester is between

200 to 260 milligrams (mg) each day. Values higher than 300 mg like clockwork are viewed as inside the diagnosable reach for proteinuria in pregnancy.

What are the side effects of protein in the urine?

Side effects show and the seriousness of proteinuria relies upon how much protein is present in the urine.

In the event that you're encountering just a minor increment, you're probably not going to have perceptible side effects. You may just realize you have an excess of protein in your urine in the event that you're regularly trying your levels.

Notwithstanding, individuals with extreme kidney harm or higher protein levels are probably going to encounter the accompanying sorts of side effects:

- Expanding in the hands, face, tummy, or feet.
- More incessant urine.
- Urine that is frothy, foamy, or effervescent.
- Oftentimes feeling queasy or retching.
- Dry or bothersome skin.
- Exhaustion.
- Muscle squeezes that will generally happen all the more frequently around evening time.

Any of the above side effects can be an indication of kidney harm. Assuming you experience any of these, look for clinical consideration right away. The best way to know whether you have proteinuria is through a urine test. This is a painless methodology that just requires a urine test at your primary care physician's office or the emergency clinic.

Contingent upon whether your condition is named present moment or long haul, you might have to keep testing for proteinuria at normal stretches. On the off chance that your test is strange, your primary care physician might suggest extra screening, for example,

- Glomerular Filtration Rate (GMR) blood test to check kidney capability.
- Imaging tests, for example, an ultrasound or CT check.
- Kidney biopsy to check for kidney harm.

How to diminish protein in the urine?

An overabundance of protein in your urine is much of the time a consequence of other basic and in some cases constant illnesses. Thus, the most ideal way to diminish protein levels is by attempting to control those contributing illnesses like kidney infection, diabetes, or even hypertension.

Contingent upon the condition(s) that are available, your doctor might prescribe various answers to better oversee them and lessen your protein levels.

For instance:

- Dietary changes, for example, diminishing sugar and salt admission might be advantageous for individuals with kidney sickness, diabetes, or hypertension.

- Drugs should be endorsed to help with controlling side effects like hypertension or glucose.
- Certain individuals might be told to follow a weight reduction plan as a component of their treatment.
- Individuals with particular sorts of kidney infection — including kidney come up short.

Focus point

As a rule, high protein levels in your urine are an indication of an irregularity. In any case, contingent upon your general health and any fundamental circumstances, having proteinuria doesn't generally mean an individual is in chronic weakness.

Fortunately, testing for the condition is a simple cycle. All the more significantly, assuming other ailments are adding to high protein levels, attempting to deal with those issues or infections is basic to rectifying any urinary awkward nature.

CHAPTER SEVEN

Stress Management's Strategies II

Stress the board procedures incorporate mental techniques, mind-body rehearses, social collaborations, time usage abilities, and normal comprehensive cures.

These techniques assist people with diminishing stress and improve general prosperity prompting a basic cheerful life.

Mental methods include changing idea designs, while mind-body rehearses integrate exercises like contemplation and yoga.

Mingling strategies center around the positive effect of social associations, and time usage methods help in focusing on errands.

Furthermore, regular comprehensive cures incorporate homegrown enhancements, fragrant healing, and unwinding procedures to ease stress.

Each approach targets various parts of stress, offering different instruments for powerful stress on the board.

You could have seen that you're more restless than expected. The American Mental Affiliation has detailed a vertical pattern in stress after the pandemic credited to different financial, socio-social, and political variables.

Mental Rebuilding

1. Mental Rebuilding

Mental rebuilding, likewise called mental reevaluating, is a procedure regularly utilized in mental conduct treatment (MCT) to supplant negative reasoning examples with positive ones. This will assist you with keeping a degree of certainty that will permit you to zero in your energy on the significant things in your day-to-day existence.

It depends on the reason that our thought process eventually concludes how we feel about conditions.

Mental rebuilding includes distinguishing the perspectives enacted during distressing circumstances and deciding whether these cycles are upsetting your inward feeling of harmony. Accordingly, it is simpler to decrease stress when we have cognizant command over our perspectives. It will likewise assist you with being more intelligent rather than promptly acting such that you will lament later.

2. Diaphragmatic Relaxing

Profound breathing utilizing the stomach has been displayed to lessen stress.

We will quite often take shallow breaths when we are anxious.

Shallow breathing influences the convergence of oxygen and carbon dioxide in the body and further demolishes the side effects of stress.

Breathing profoundly for a couple of moments decreases the level of the stress chemical cortisol in our blood, and furthermore adds to bring down pulse levels, and pulses. Profound breathing likewise further develops a resistant framework working and gives a sensation of unwinding and general prosperity.

3. Conduct Initiation

Social initiation is a piece of mental conduct treatment where we intentionally decide to do exercises that make us blissful and assist us with overseeing stress. It may very well be **meeting with our friends and family, going out traveling, seeking after our side interests, and taking a solid eating regimen.**

Keeping ourselves occupied in satisfying and significant exercises leaves us with no time for negative contemplations and stress. Moreover, remaining in an unpleasant climate and failing to address it will just increase feelings of anxiety.

Mind-Body Procedures

1. Yoga

Yoga is one of the unwinding procedures that bring the physical and mental parts of health together. Hatha yoga is the most regularly drilled procedure for stress decrease. It stresses breathing and stance.

Moreover, it constructs major areas of strength for between 3 parts of well-being; body, brain, and soul.

This actual work lessens muscle stress, upgrades actual equilibrium, further develops rest quality, and loosens up the brain. At last, we figure out how to effectively control unpleasant circumstances.

2. Reflection

Reflection is one of the oldest strategies for impeding the wellsprings of stress and working on mental honesty. It implies **remaining still and quiet for a couple of moments** in a peaceful climate. You can inhale profoundly and center around your breathing developments during the meeting or you can write in a reflection diary.

Reflection helps in loosening up the psyche, expanding fixation, learning inward harmony, and diminishing stress. Additionally, it keeps you quiet even after your meeting is finished. Thus, you will generally remain tranquil in your regular routine.

3. Judo

Judo, likewise called contemplation moving, is a Chinese procedure that **includes slow and ceaseless body developments.** It was at first presented as a military craftsmanship strategy.

Yet, presently it is polished to adapt to stress and lead a sound way of life.
The delicate change starts with one stance then onto the next interface psyche and body. In this way, it gives a feeling of inward harmony, serenity, and equilibrium

throughout everyday life. Kendo is additionally utilized for other medical conditions like coronary illness, joint shortcomings, and hypertension.

4. Qi Gong

Qi Gong, an old Chinese practice, encapsulates the craft of developing fundamental life energy, known as Qi or Chi, to advance comprehensive prosperity. Established in customary Chinese medication and reasoning, Qi Gong coordinates various strategies like actual stances, breathing methods, and mental concentration to adjust the body's energy stream, improving physical, mental, and profound wellbeing.

Beginnings and Reasoning:

Starting in China a long time back, Qi Gong drew motivation from Taoism, Confucianism, and Chinese medication. The training spins around the conviction that a reasonable Qi stream is crucial for well-being, with disturbances prompting disease. Qi Gong means to orchestrate this energy, cultivating essentialness, internal harmony, and life span. Today, there are numerous ways of getting confirmed in QiGong practice.

Objectives of Qi Gong:

- **Energy Development:** Qi Gong centers around upgrading the body's Qi stream, advancing essentialness, endurance, and energy levels.

- **Stress Decrease:** Through delicate developments and breath control, Qi Gong diminishes stress , uneasiness, and strain, initiating a condition of unwinding.

- **Equilibrium and Coordination**: Qi Gong activities to further develop equilibrium, coordination, and adaptability, improving actual steadiness and forestalling falls.

- **Torment The management:** The training is viable in overseeing persistent agony conditions, advancing mending, and decreasing uneasiness.

- **Profound Prosperity:** Qi Gong cultivates close-to-home equilibrium, helping with dealing with feelings, lessening emotional episodes, and improving mental clearness.

Type of Qi Gong

Clinical Qi Gong

Centers around mending explicit sicknesses and awkward nature by guiding Qi to impacted body parts, advancing recuperation and prosperity.

Daoist QiGong

Established in Daoist reasoning, this type underlines profound development, reflection, and blending with the regular progression of Qi.

Confucian Qi Gong

Consolidates moral and moral standards, holding back nothing, temperance development, and amicable social connections.

Shaolin Qi Gong

Gotten from Shaolin hand-to-hand fighting, this training underscores functional preparation, mental concentration, and battle strategies, advancing in general health and self-preservation abilities.

Advantages and disadvantages of Qi Gong:

Advantages:

1. Upgrades generally energy levels and essentialness.
2. It Lessens stress, and tension, and advances unwinding.
3. Further develop equilibrium, coordination, and adaptability.
4. Viable in overseeing ongoing torment and advancing recuperating.

5. Improves profound prosperity and mental lucidity.

Disadvantages:

1. Requires reliable practice for huge advantages.
2. May require direction from experienced educators for legitimate methods.
3. Not a handy solution; slow advancement is frequently noticed.
4. May not suit people searching for focused energy exercises.
5. Restricted logical examination contrasted with standard treatments.

5. Directed Symbolism

We as a whole have envisioned our fantasy vacations, accomplishing our objectives, and doing things we love, correct? Directed symbolism is like that. It is a stress-help strategy in which we **envision a serene landscape,** the urinating of birds, the streaming of streams, the blowing of the breeze, relieving temperature, and entrancing scents.

This assists us with removing our consideration from the stress in our daily existences and pondering the positive parts of life.

It will likewise give us a new restart which permits us to distinctively get things done.

Mingling Strategies

1. Join a club

Finding a gathering of people with similar interests and side interests as you are a magnificent method for managing the stress that accompanies dejection and separation. Taking these new risks for connection additionally opens entryways and more open doors for you.

Regardless of what you are, a bibliophile, a sportsperson, or a performer, you can find individuals who are enthusiastic about similar stuff. These clubs or coteries can be tracked down over the web, around your home or working environment, or you can make one yourself.

2. Selflessness

Philanthropy is the ethical act of being caring and focusing on the requirements of others over your own. Philanthropic behavior like **chipping in at the neighborhood destitute sanctuary, adding to a magnanimous establishment, supporting social liberties,** and so on can assist with easing stress by giving a feeling of motivation to your life.

You can meet other charitable people along these lines and begin long-lasting fellowships. You can likewise associate with people needing your assistance and have a constructive outcome in their lives.

3. Welcome Loved ones Over

What could be preferable over time spent in the organization of friends and family? You can welcome your loved ones over for supper or lunch, and plan fun exercises like pretenses, table games, film evenings, or just a solid discussion.

Stress influences life like a sluggish toxin.

Investing energy with true and caring individuals can end up being a remedy and assist you with defeating burnout.

Time Usage Strategies

1. Make a Plan for the day

One of the foundation propensities for compelling using time productively is **recording your day-to-day undertakings** and dealing with them individually.

At the point when every one of your responsibilities and errands is organized and focused on in view of direness and significance, less investment is spent stressing and worrying about.

2. Separate It into More modest Advances

Frequently, stress takes over at whatever point we have doled out a significant undertaking. Here, the arrangement is to **separate a definitive objective into little objectives** and work towards them without contemplating everything out and out.

Going through more modest advances gives a sensation of achievement, supports certainty, and fortifies us to effortlessly accomplish the end product. In actuality, attempting to accomplish the fundamental objective in one go can prompt tension and disappointment.

3. Figure out how to Say No

Something else we become fretted over is taking others' weights on ourselves. Being thoughtful, useful, and steady is pleasant however not to the detriment of your psychological wellness. You ought to possibly express yes to the undertakings when you have time and little exertion is required.

Figuring out how to say no is a fundamental stage in the act of taking care of oneself. It assists us with focusing on ourselves, esteeming ourselves, and caring more for our psychological and actual well-being.

Comprehensive Procedures - Elective Wellbeing

1. Spices

Complex answers for stress and different health concerns. Dissimilar to their drug partners, spices furnish an agreeable collaboration with the body, tending to the side effects as well as the fundamental reasons for stress and plenty of different diseases. Here is a nitty gritty investigation of their noteworthy advantages:

Alleviating Stress and Sensory System Backing:

-Kidneys: Dandelion and Parsley, perceived diuretics, support kidney detoxification by upgrading ideal working and decreasing poison collection, advancing kidney wellbeing. This, thus, eases weight on the body's filtration framework and supports a sound sensory system.

-Cardiovascular Wellbeing: Hawthorn, adored for its cardiovascular advantages, assists lower with high bleeding stress, upgrading heart health normally. Overseeing stress reaction, adds to a decent sensory system, advancing in general prosperity.

-Regenerative Wellbeing: Chamomile, with its relieving properties, facilitates period cramps, offering delicate help during the monthly cycle. Bother, wealthy in supplements, upholds generally speaking regenerative well-being, guaranteeing an amicable hormonal equilibrium, crucial for stress the board. A few spices utilized related to different procedures like needle therapy could likewise assist with curing normal diseases like fibroids.

-Muscle and Joint Wellbeing: Demon's Paw, famous for its calming properties, lightens gout, and gives help from joint torment. Arnica, a characteristic muscle relaxant, targets muscle snugness and back torment, helping with unwinding and versatility, fundamental for stress alleviation.

-Circulatory Help: Ginkgo Biloba, a spice praised for its vasodilatory impacts, guarantees better blood course, fighting issues like varicose veins and upgrading general circulatory effectiveness. Further developed flow helps with stress decrease by advancing a quiet and consistent sensory system.

-Mental and Profound Equilibrium: Lavender, a sweet-smelling spice, and Ashwagandha, an adaptogenic force to be reckoned with, lessen tension and stress during pregnancy and in regular day-to-day existence, advancing close-to-homeprosperity. They calm the sensory system, offering transient help from stress and upgrading general emotional well-being.

-**Clear,** Sound Skin: Burdock Root, with its purging properties, targets hormonal skin inflammation, advancing clear and brilliant skin normally. Clear skin frequently reflects internal equilibrium and can fundamentally add to decreased feelings of anxiety.

-Antifungal Safeguard: Tea Tree Oil, eminent for its antifungal properties, actually handles contagious contaminations, offering alleviation without the unforgiving symptoms of customary prescriptions. Reducing skin issues adds to general prosperity, supporting stress on the management.

Utilizing Natural Medication

1. Moxibustion:

Types of Moxibustion:

- **Direct Moxibustion:** Moxa cones or sticks are put straightforwardly on the skin.
- **Backhanded Moxibustion:** Moxa sticks are held over the skin, with a layer of defensive substance like ginger or salt to forestall consumption.

Where to Purchase Moxa Sticks:

Moxa sticks are accessible at homegrown stores, needle therapy facilities, and online stages gaining practical experience in conventional Chinese medication supplies.

The most effective method to Utilize Moxa Sticks:

- Light the moxa stick and hold it near the needle therapy point, tenderly moving it in roundabout movements.

Benefits:

- Moxibustion improves blood flow, helps the insusceptible framework, and lightens torment. It is frequently utilized for ongoing circumstances and contraceptive medical conditions.

Homegrown Teas:

Utilization:

- Chamomile tea helps with unwinding and advances better rest.
- Ginger tea mitigates the stomach-related framework and decreases sickness.
- Lavender tea helps in stress alleviation and prompts tranquility.

Instructions to Mix Home grown Teas:

- Steep 1-2 teaspoons of dried spices in steaming hot water for 5-10 minutes

Benefits:

- Natural teas are rich in cancer prevention agents, advance unwinding, help absorption, and lift the safe framework.

Home-grown Enhancements:

Utilization:

- Ginseng supplements upgrade energy and imperativeness.
- Turmeric supplements have calming properties.
- Echinacea supplements support the resistant framework.

Instructions to Take Natural Enhancements:

- Follow the proposed portion on the item name.

Benefits:

- Natural enhancements offer designated help for different health worries, from energy improvement to resistant framework support.
- **Homegrown Colors:**

Utilization:

- St. John's Wort color helps with temperament balance.
- Milk Thorn color upholds liver well-being.
- Valerian color advances unwinding and rest.

Step-by-step instructions to Utilize Natural Colors:

- Blend the suggested measurements in with water and drink.

Benefits:

- Homegrown colors offer concentrated natural advantages, helping with explicit medical problems like uneasiness, liver detoxification, and rest issues.

Natural Culinary Pleasures:
Use:

- Basil adds spice to dishes and has antimicrobial properties.
- Turmeric supports resistance and makes calming impacts.

- Cilantro supports detoxification and adds a reviving taste.

The most effective method to Consolidate Spices in Cooking:

- Add new or dried spices to soups, mixed greens, and principal dishes.

Benefits:

- Culinary spices improve taste, give fundamental supplements, and deal with different medical advantages, from insusceptible help to supporting processing.

2. Gua Sha

Gua Sha, beginning from conventional Chinese medication, is a stress-easing method that includes tenderly scratching the skin to upgrade blood dissemination and advance the energy stream. Dissimilar to traditional strategies, Gua Sha gives comprehensive health through its normal, painless methodology.

Step-by-step instructions to Utilize Gua Sha:

- **Set up Your Skin:** Apply a facial oil or serum to make a smooth surface.
- **Hold at a Point:** Hold the Gua Sha instrument at a 15-degree point against your skin. This might change as you proceed with your

Gua Sha excursion and you learn new methods.

- **Skim with Care:** Tenderly coast the device in vertical and outward movements, following your facial shapes.

- **Clean your devices:** Consistently end your meeting by cleaning the apparatuses you use to keep away from any soil or bacterial gathering.

Mix into Skincare Schedule:

- Integrate Gua Sha prior to applying lotion for best outcomes.

- Improve its adequacy by coordinating it into your ordinary skincare routine. This will assist you with accomplishing better and better facial highlights.

Contrasting Gua Sha with Different Apparatuses:

- **Versus Jade Rollers:** Gua Sha apparatuses offer more exact plots for a designated facial back rub.
- **Versus NuFace Gadgets:** Gua Sha is non-electric, giving a manual, customized insight.

Investigating Tones, Shapes, and Materials:

- Gua Sha devices come in different materials like rose quartz, jade, and bian stone, each accepted to have exceptional recuperating properties.

- Pick a shape that accommodates your facial shapes easily for ideal outcomes.

Significant Contemplations:

- **Control is Vital:** Stay away from inordinate use to forestall skin aggravation.
- **Choices:** Facial back rub and stress point massage can supplement Gua Sha for a balanced methodology.
- **Certificate:** No affirmation is expected for individual use, making it open to everybody.
- **Cleaning:** Keep up with cleanliness by cleaning the instrument with a gentle cleanser

and warm water after each utilization.

All-encompassing Medical advantages:

- **Facial Thinning:** Gua Sha helps in conditioning facial muscles, advancing a chiseled appearance.
- **Wrinkle Decrease:** Normal use lessens scarcely discernible differences and kinks, advancing young skin.
- **Cellulite Decrease:** Gua Sha supports animating lymphatic seepage, lessening the presence of cellulite.

3. Tui Na

Tui Na, established in conventional Chinese medication, remains a signal of all-encompassing recuperating, zeroing in on the body's energy pathways to ease stress and agony.

This old remedial back rub strategy incorporates cadenced manipulating, squeezing, and extending to adjust the body's energy stream, advancing unwinding, and reducing muscle strain.

While Tui Na is famous for its viability in overseeing stress and different torments, it's quite significant that people with low agony resilience could find it marginally awkward because of its extreme tension.

Methods Utilized in Tui Na:

- Rolling.
- Working.
- Squeezing.
- Extending.
- Percussion.

Conceivable Incidental Effects:

- Transitory touchiness.
- Exhaustion.
- Swelling (intriguing).

Advantages of Tui Na:

- Stress alleviation and unwinding.
- Torment the board.
- Further developed course.
- Improved adaptability and versatility.

Contrasting Tui Na with Different Strategies:

- **Tui Na versus Swedish Back rub:** Tui Na includes further, designated stress, zeroing in on energy pathways, while Swedish back rub basically utilizes long, skimming strokes for unwinding.

- **Tui Na versus Thai Back Rub:** Tui Na utilizes serious squeezing and playing, while Thai back rub consolidates yoga-like stretches and delicate shaking movements.

- **Tui Na versus Chiropractic:** Tui Na accentuates manual control of delicate tissues and stress point massage focuses, appearing differently in relation to chiropractic's attention to spinal changes.

4. Needle therapy

Needle therapy is the antiquated Chinese act of embedding slim needles at explicit body focuses to alleviate torment. In late practice, it has been utilized to stress the management with variable outcomes. Western professionals accept that this strategy animates nerves, muscles, and connective tissue and alleviates stress in aggravated body parts. Others even claim that it tends to be helped by weaning off persistent vices like smoking.

Needle therapy's comprehensive nature tends to the actual side effects as well as the main drivers of stress, advancing in general prosperity. One critical perspective to note is the recurrence of meetings. For stress, the board, customary needle therapy meetings, commonly one time each week or fortnightly, can yield critical advantages.

Contrasting Needle Therapy and Different Strategies:

- **Needle therapy as opposed to Measuring:** While needle therapy includes needles to animate the energy stream, measuring utilizes pull cups to advance blood course and reduce muscle stress.

- **Needle therapy versus Reflexology:** Needle therapy targets explicit meridian focuses, while reflexology applies strain to reflex zones on the feet, hands, and ears to advance unwinding and balance in relating body parts.

- **Needle therapy versus Botox:** Needle therapy advances normal recuperating by adjusting energy, while Botox includes infusions to deaden muscles, diminishing kinks for a brief time. Needle therapy's all-encompassing methodology centers around generally speaking prosperity instead of corrective improvements.

- **Needle therapy versus Dry Needling:** Needle therapy, established in antiquated Chinese medication, plans to address physical and close-to-homeuneven characteristics. Dry needling, a cutting-edge restorative method, includes embedding slight needles into trigger focuses to reduce strong agony and distress. While both use needles, needle therapy's comprehensive methodology includes a more extensive range of health concerns, offering a thorough answer for generally speaking prosperity. Dry needling, conversely, explicitly targets confined muscle issues, making it reasonable for specific outer muscle issues.

Find the exceptional flexibility of needle therapy in tending to a huge number of medical problems:

1. Going bald

- Needle therapy animates blood course to hair follicles, empowering normal hair development and forestalling further misfortune.
- By tending to hidden lopsided characteristics, needle therapy upholds generally scalp wellbeing, advancing thicker, better hair.

2. Dizziness

- Needle therapy orchestrates the body's energy stream, settling inward ear unsettling influences that cause dizziness.

- Standard needle therapy meetings have been displayed to diminish the recurrence and force of dizziness episodes, working on general personal satisfaction.

- It can likewise help tinnitus by and large since it re-balances the inward ear issues.

3. Spinal Stenosis

- Needle therapy offers to torment the board for spinal stenosis, focusing on unambiguous focuses to ease distress and further develop portability.

- Through delicate excitement, needle therapy loosens up muscles around the impacted region, lessening the strain on the spine.
- This additionally influences different joints like the shoulders and hips accordingly expanding alleviation for tight joint muscles.

4. Neck Agony and Sciatica

- Needle therapy mitigates muscle stress in the neck and lower back, giving help from persistent agony and uneasiness.
- By delivering endorphins, needle therapy advances unwinding,

diminishing nerve bothering, and facilitating sciatic nerve torment.

5. Chemical Unevenness

- Needle therapy reestablishes hormonal equilibrium by controlling the endocrine framework, and resolving issues, for example, unpredictable periods, fibroids, state of mind swings, and weariness.

- By focusing on unambiguous focuses connected with hormonal capability, needle therapy advances concordance inside the body, lightening the side effects of awkwardness.

6. Tension

- Needle therapy meetings advance close-to-homeprosperity by adjusting energy and lessening stress chemicals like cortisol.
- The quieting impact of needle therapy mitigates tension side effects, upgrading mental clearness and profound soundness.

7. Gout

- Needle therapy enacts the body's regular recuperating components, diminishing aggravation and facilitating torment related to gout assaults.
- Customary needle therapy therapies can assist with overseeing uric corrosive levels, decreasing the recurrence and force of gout episodes.

8. Stomach Issues

- Needle therapy resolves stomach-related issues by controlling gastrointestinal motility and lessening irritation in the stomach lining.

- By improving blood flow to the stomach-related organs, needle therapy advances mending and lets side effects free from gastritis, heartburn, acid reflux, and even kidney stones.

9. Muscle touchiness

- Needle therapy demonstrates profound gainfulness for mitigating muscle bunches and irritation. Focusing on unambiguous triggers loosens up muscles, and delivers strain.

- Needle therapy may not give significant help to cutting-edge or extreme instances of carpal passage disorder. While it can assist with dealing with specific side effects like less than overwhelming torment or uneasiness briefly, different medicines, for example, wrist braces or medical procedures, may be more viable in tending to the main driver of the condition.

Aftercare and What's in store Following Needle therapy Meetings?

After a needle therapy meeting, it's fundamental to comprehend what's in store and how to deal with any vibes that might emerge. This is what you need to put into notice:

Sensations After Needle Therapy

- **Impermanent Uneasiness:** It's normal to encounter gentle delicacy or irritation at the needle therapy focus. This is a typical reaction and normally dies down in the span of a little while.

- **Expanded Side effects:** at times, your side effects could briefly deteriorate before they get to the next level. This peculiarity is known as a "recuperating emergency" and is a positive sign that your body is responding to the treatment.

What to Do:

- **Remain Hydrated:** Appropriate hydration is essential to assist your body with flushing out poisons and keeping up with by and large prosperity.

- **Rest:** Permit your body time to recuperate and change. Sufficient rest upholds the mending system.

- **Delicate Developments:** Take part in delicate developments or stretches to advance the course and keep up with the advantages of needle therapy.

- **Keep away from Overexertion:** Cease from exhausting exercises or hard work following a meeting to forestall strain.

- **Keep away from extreme temperature changes:** This implies that showering with freezing or exceptionally heated water might make the recuperation of the body slower.

Correspondence with Your Acupuncturist

Assuming that you experience serious or delayed distress, or on the other hand on the off chance that your side effects deteriorate fundamentally, make it a point to your acupuncturist. They can give direction and change your treatment plan if important. Understanding the aftercare and what's in store present needle therapy is vital to expanding the advantages of this all-encompassing treatment. It's memorable that brief distress or expanded side effects are in many cases a characteristic piece of the recuperating system, flagging that your body is on the way to working on prosperity.

Grasping the Expenses and Planning Needle Therapy Meetings

While considering needle therapy as an all-encompassing way to deal with well-being, it's fundamental to know about the normal expenses related to these remedial meetings. The cost of needle therapy can differ in view of elements, for example, area, specialist experience, and the span of the meeting. By and large, a needle therapy meeting in the US can go from $15 to $300 per meeting, with beginning discussions frequently being somewhat higher because of the complete evaluation included. It likewise incredibly differs depending upon the kind of needle therapy that will be directed.

Booking a needle therapy arrangement is a direct interaction intended to oblige your comfort. Start by exploring authorized and respectable acupuncturists in your space. A large number have official sites or postings where you can track down their contact data. Connect with your preferred acupuncturist through telephone or email to examine your interests and timetable a reasonable arrangement time.

During the underlying interview, the acupuncturist will direct an intensive evaluation, examining your clinical history, side effects, and health objectives. This thorough comprehension permits the professional to fit the needle therapy meetings to your particular necessities, guaranteeing a customized and successful way to deal with your health and prosperity. These variables will direct the length of the visit since certain cases might be more confounded than others. Keep in mind, open correspondence with your acupuncturist is vital to an effective and remunerating needle therapy experience.

5. Fragrant healing

Fragrant healing, a characteristic cure established in the quintessence of plants, offers a comprehensive way to deal with stress decrease. Breathing in sweet-smelling rejuvenating ointments enacts the cerebrum's personal habitats, advancing unwinding and facilitating stress. Aromas like jasmine, lavender, chamomile, and citrus oils have quieting properties, making them viable stress busters. Fragrance-based treatment diffusers, accessible in different plans, scatter these restorative scents all through living spaces, establishing peaceful conditions ideal for unwinding.

The most effective method to Get Diffusers and Oils: Fragrance-based treatment instruments, including diffusers and medicinal balms, are promptly open on the web or at neighborhood health stores. Diffusers come in ultrasonic, nebulizing, and heat-based variations, with easy-to-use highlights. Natural oils can be bought separately or in sets, offering a great many scents to suit individual inclinations.

Lessening stress: The Science Behind Fragrant Healing: When breathed in, sweet-smelling atoms enter the circulation system, affecting the limbic framework, which controls feelings and lower stress reactions. Natural balms like lavender and bergamot trigger the arrival of synapses, advancing unwinding. Fragrant healing has shown viability rates in diminishing stress and uneasiness, which concentrates on featuring its positive effect on mental prosperity. Integrating fragrance-based treatment into everyday schedules can essentially upgrade stress-the-board endeavors, giving a fragrant pathway to serenity and equilibrium.

6. Hypnotherapy

On the off chance that nothing is by all accounts working for you, hypnotherapy can be a powerful choice. Hypnotherapy is a clinical stress-the-board strategy that **utilizes spellbinding to direct you into a loose and centered mental state.**

Hypnotherapy **includes your cognizant and subliminal** as well as utilizing coordination among psyche and body to manage sorrow and forestall ongoing stress. It offers a groundbreaking way to deal with overseeing stress. Taking advantage of the unwinding reaction gives a strong remedy for the impacts of upsetting occasions. Through directed meetings, people learn sound ways of exploring life's difficulties, helping with stress decrease and profound equilibrium. During entrancing, the brain enters a condition of profound concentration and receptivity, empowering **the arrival of endorphins**, the body's normal stress relievers. The interaction includes a gifted specialist directing clients through unwinding methods, and getting to the psyche brain to address basic stress triggers.

System and Adequacy

Hypnotherapy meetings ordinarily include acceptance, developing, idea, and arousing stages. The enlistment stage incites a condition of unwinding, making ready for a more profound subliminal investigation. Extending methods improve this dazed state, guaranteeing receptivity to positive ideas. Advisors utilize customized scripts, directing clients towards better reactions to stressors. Logical examinations feature hypnotherapy's viability in reducing stress-related side effects, making it a confided-in strategy for dealing with the impacts of stress.

Planning a Meeting

It is easy to Timetable a hypnotherapy arrangement. Legitimate experts can be tracked down through web-based catalogs or proposals. Most advisors offer advantageous internet booking choices, guaranteeing openness. Meetings can occur in advisors' workplaces or basically, giving adaptability to suit individual inclinations and timetables.

Embracing hypnotherapy isn't just about alleviating stress; it's tied in with engaging people to answer life's difficulties in better, more versatile ways. By encouraging unwinding, tending to stress sets off, and advancing the body's normal stress help components, hypnotherapy remains a reference point of all-encompassing prosperity, directing people toward enduring quiet and versatility.

7. Measuring

Measuring treatment, an old all-encompassing practice has acquired gigantic ubiquity for its stress-easing advantages and by and large health impacts. By making attractions on the skin's surface, measuring **animates bloodstream**, advancing unwinding, and lessening stress. To play out this treatment, specific instruments like cups, commonly made of glass, plastic, or silicone, are utilized. The cups could likewise have various tones implying various degrees of force in stress levels. The system includes making a vacuum inside the cup and putting an unambiguous focus on the body.

This is the way measuring treatment helps different circumstances:

Scoliosis

- Measuring treatment targets muscle irregular characteristics related to scoliosis, advancing better arrangement and decreasing uneasiness.

- By loosening up tense muscles around the spine, measuring adds to a further developed pose and decreases the burden on the impacted regions.

Muscle Strain

- Competitors frequently experience muscle strain; measuring treatment series up the recuperating system by improving blood course to impacted muscles.

- The treatment assists discharge with muscling bunches and stress, supporting quicker recuperation and empowering competitors to quickly get back to maximized operation.

Neck Agony

- Measuring treatment lightens neck torment by lessening muscle solidness and aggravation in the cervical locale.

- By advancing unwinding and invigorating blood stream, measuring facilitates muscle fits and improves neck adaptability, prompting dependable help.

Back Agony

- Ongoing back torment frequently results from muscle snugness; measuring treatment tends to this by releasing muscles and further developing adaptability.

- The treatment's pull impact helps discharge caught poisons, diminishing aggravation and agony, and giving genuinely necessary solace to people experiencing back torment.

Muscle Bunches

- Measuring treatment definitively targets muscle hitches, applying delicate strain to deliver stress and reestablish regular muscle capability.
- By upgrading oxygen and supplement supply to tied muscles, measuring supports dissolving hitches, advancing moderate muscle unwinding, and decreasing distress.

Cellulite Decrease

- Measuring treatment supports dissemination and lymphatic waste, successfully separating cellulite stores underneath the skin.
- Further developed bloodstream revives the skin, advancing collagen creation, and upgrading

skin surface and tone, prompting a smoother, firmer appearance.

Types of Measuring:

• Streak Measuring

Brief attractions to fortify energy streams. This strategy is great for people looking for rejuvenating support without the drawn-out pull of customary measuring techniques.

• Lip Measuring

Uses more modest cups, frequently for facial regions. By upgrading dissemination and advancing lymphatic waste, this procedure adds to a characteristic facelift, lessening puffiness, and reestablishing facial essentialness.

• Foot Measuring

Target stress point massage focuses on the feet. This procedure advances unwinding as well as supports generally speaking health by invigorating imperative reflex zones, upgrading the energy stream all through the body.

• Facial Measuring

Improves facial flow and skin imperativeness. By expanding flow, it advances collagen creation, decreases barely recognizable differences, and reestablishes a young gleam. This harmless strategy revives the skin's normal imperativeness.

- **Fire Measuring**

Fire measuring includes momentarily lighting a fire inside the cup before applying it to the skin. This method makes a vacuum impact, advancing profound tissue unwinding and empowering the body's normal recuperating reactions. Fire measuring is adored for its conventional remedial advantages.

- **Wet Measuring**

Wet measuring, otherwise called "Hijama," includes making slight cuts on the skin to eliminate a limited quantity of blood. This technique is accepted to detoxify the body, advancing an equilibrium of natural liquids and working with the end of poisons. Wet measuring is frequently pursued for its potential all-encompassing medical advantages.

Method:

• Arrangement of Cups

During measuring treatment, uncommonly planned cups are decisively put on unambiguous marks of the body called measuring treatment focuses. The term of the situation differs, regularly enduring between 5 to 30 minutes. These focuses are carefully picked in light of the singular's affliction or concern, lining up with the body's meridian lines. This exact situation guarantees that the treatment focuses on the main driver of distress, advancing a fair progression of energy all through the body.

- **Mark Appearance**

After the cups are eliminated, brief imprints show up on the skin, looking like round wounds. These imprints are a characteristic reaction to the treatment and demonstrate the arrival of poisons and stale energy from the body. Even though they could seem extreme, these imprints are innocuous and generally blur within a couple of days. They act as apparent verification of the treatment's adequacy, displaying the body's mending cycle in real life.

- **Mending Surged increase**

To improve the recuperating system of these imprints, different regular cures can be utilized. Applying balms like arnica, famous for its calming properties, helps with lessening staining and accelerating recuperation. The utilization of these effective arrangements guarantees that the skin recuperates without a hitch, limiting any leftover indications of measuring treatment.

Meeting Recurrence

Individualized Approach

The recurrence of measuring treatment meetings is exceptionally individualized. It changes in light of the singular's particular condition, the seriousness of side effects, and their general health objectives. A talented specialist surveys the individual extensively, fitting the recurrence of meetings to successfully address their interesting requirements.

Normal Frequencies

Numerous people track down predictable alleviation through week after week or fortnightly measuring treatment medicines. Normal meetings guarantee that the remedial advantages are maintained, taking into consideration the progressing torment of the board, stress decrease, and generally speaking prosperity. The recurrence is changed in light of the singular's advancement, guaranteeing that they get the ideal degree of care all through their mending process.

Points of interest and Contemplations

From a monetary viewpoint, the expense of measuring treatment can change generally. It is impacted by elements like the advisor's skill and the geological area of the training. In the US, the standard charge for briefly measuring meetings commonly falls within the scope of $50 to $100. This interest in your prosperity gives admittance to a revered recuperating strategy customized to address explicit health concerns.

Notwithstanding, similarly as with any remedial procedure, measuring treatment accompanies its contemplations. While the treatment offers huge alleviation, it's vital to note that it could cause gentle uneasiness during the meeting. Furthermore, transitory imprints might show up on the skin because of the pull impact of the cups. These imprints, frequently looking like roundabout injuries, are innocuous and typically blur within a couple of days. This normal event is a demonstration of the treatment's viability, showing the arrival of poisons and stale energy from the body.

To guarantee a protected and successful measuring experience, **counseling a prepared and experienced practitioner** is significant. Their skill ensures an agreeable meeting as well as guarantees that the treatment adjusts agreeably with your body's energy stream. Focusing on your security and prosperity, a gifted expert will modify the treatment, making fundamental changes following stress levels and strategies given your singular requirements. The professional will likewise express a few ideas on what to do after the meeting to expand the impacts of measuring.

Regularly Clarified some pressing issues

Our health mentor group has gathered and responded to a rundown of inquiries connected with the stress of the management's procedures that are most often asked by our perusers.

What are the 5 stresses of the management's methods?

The best stress the management's strategies incorporate;

- **Mental procedures:** These include intentionally controlling your body to adapt to stress.

- **Body-mind strategies:** These include activities to quiet your brain and accomplish a condition of internal harmony.

- **Mingling procedures:** These include getting help from your gathering to light up the temperament.

- **Time usage methods:** These strategies help in the counteraction of stress-creating circumstances in any case.

- **All-encompassing Methods:** These include health proficient directed treatments to decrease stress.

What are the 3 systems for adapting to stress?

The 3 systems for adapting to stress are actual activity, consuming a solid eating regimen, and connecting for social help.

The 4 A's of stress help are:

- **Avoid:** You can keep away from a ton of stressors basically by saying no, declining solicitations to meet with individuals who channel your energy, and assuming command over your environmental elements.

- **Alter:** Where conceivable, attempt to adjust the circumstances that adversely influence your emotional well-being. Assuming that implies removing individuals, make it happen.

- **Acknowledge:** A few circumstances are irredeemable. We can acknowledge them as they are and continue.
- **Adjust:** Now and again, you would need to adjust to persistent stress by having an impact on your points of view and assumptions.

What are the four C's of stress for the management?

The four C's of stress management, created by the English advisor specialist Dr. Sarmila Sinha, are as per the following:

- **Calm:** The most important move towards stress alleviation is deferring reaction to distressing circumstances. Just once you are certain that you are not generally wrecked with feelings are you permitted to answer and act?

- **Clarity:** This step includes gathering data and new points of view toward upsetting circumstances to go with additional educated choices.
- **Choice:** This step allows you to understand that you generally have command over your activities and you can decide to answer with outrage or consideration.
- **Change:** You will see a substantial change in your life when you follow the three stages.

Summary

This research recognizes that individuals have been encountering stress for quite a longtime. However, its occurrence has expanded dramatically as of late. Consequently, stress is a typical present-day life issue. Be that as it may, this normal issue gives way to an inadequate way of life. The time has come to assume control over the matter and manage your stress. Above, we made sense of a few simple methods that can assist you with dealing with it and defeat your time in this life.

Synopsis

The critical message in these books:
Wellbeing is a fragile difficult exercise, and persistent pressure can without much of a stretch upset that equilibrium by harming our insusceptible and sensory systems. In the most pessimistic scenarios, persistent pressure can add to the beginning and fuel diseases like MS, malignant growth, and ALS. It's simply by retribution with our undesirable survival techniques, horrendous character qualities, and quelled feelings that we can battle pressure and recover our well-being.

Noteworthy counsel: Figure out how to communicate your indignation better.

There's an odd conundrum with regard to outrage: quelling it can lead to physiological issues, yet so can communicating it through shouting, yelling, and hitting things. Truth be told, these works of art, innocent approaches to carrying on are approaches to staying away from the genuine encounter of fury. The key is rather to permit yourself to feel outrage however not erupt accordingly. All things being equal, sit serenely and let the fury consume you.